NEW ENGLAND

Richard Nelson's plays include *Misha's Party* (co-written with Alexander Gelman for the Royal Shakespeare Company and the Moscow Art Theatre), *Columbus and the Discovery of Japan* (RSC), *Two Shakespearean Actors* (RSC, Lincoln Center Theatre), *Some Americans Abroad* (RSC, Lincoln Center Theatre), *Sensibility and Sense* (American Playhouse Television), *Principia Scriptoriae* (RSC, Manhattan Theatre Club), *Between East and West*, *Life Sentences*, *The Return of Pinocchio*, *Rip Van Winkle or The Works*, *The Vienna Notes*, *An American Comedy*. Radio plays include *Languages Spoken Here* (BBC Radio 3), *Eating Words* (Radio 4 and the World Service), *Roots in Water* (Radio 3), *Advice to Eastern Europe* (Radio 4), and *The American Wife* (Radio 3). Television play: *End of a Sentence* (American Playhouse); film: *Ethan Frome*. Among his awards are the prestigious Lila Wallace Readers' Digest Award in 1991, a London *Time Out* Award, two Obies, two Giles Cooper Awards, a Guggenheim Fellowship, two Rockefeller playwriting grants and two National Endowment for the Arts playwriting fellowships.

NEW ENGLAND

NEW ENGLAND

RICHARD NELSON

faber and faber
LONDON · BOSTON

First published in Great Britain in 1994
by Faber and Faber Limited
3 Queen Square London WC1N 3AU

Photoset by Parker Typesetting Service, Leicester
Printed in England by Clays Ltd, St Ives plc

Richard Nelson is hereby identified as author of this work in
accordance with Section 77 of the Copyright, Designs and
Patents Act 1988

ISBN 0–571–17510–4

Printed in the United States of America

For Patricia Macnaughton
and
Peter Franklin

CHARACTERS

HARRY BAKER: sixties, professor of music at Dutchess
Community College, New York State
ALFRED BAKER: sixties, Harry's brother
GEMMA BAKER: 39, Harry's oldest child
ELIZABETH BAKER: 37, Harry's other daughter
PAUL BAKER: 32, Harry's son
SOPHIE: 41, Paul's wife
ALICE BERRY: 54, Harry's girlfriend
TOM BERRY: 40, Alice's ex-brother-in-law

All the characters are English except for Sophie,
who was born in France.

The play takes place in a farmhouse in Western Connecticut, just
across the border from New York State. The time is the present.

New England was first performed by The Royal Shakespeare Company on 23 November 1994 at the Pit in the Barbican, London. The cast was as follows:

ALICE BERRY	Angela Thorne
ALFRED/HARRY BAKER	David Burke
TOM BERRY	Mick Ford
ELIZABETH BAKER	Selina Cadell
PAUL BAKER	Duncan Bell
GEMMA BAKER	Diana Hardcastle
SOPHIE BAKER	Annie Corbier

Director	Peter Gill
Designer	Hayden Griffin
Musical Director	Terry Davis
Producer	Lynda Farran
Stage Manager	Jane Pole
Deputy Stage Manager	Caroline Beale
Assistant Stage Manager	Lynda Snowden

SCENE I

A small room on the ground floor, which serves as a study. Late afternoon; a Friday.

HARRY BAKER, *sixties, sits at a desk. On the desk is a CD player and a row of CDs – all classical; Harry is a professor of music at the local community college. He reads or looks through a book as he listens to music – Debussy's* The Girl with the Flaxen Hair *(played on the violin), begins with the scene.*

After a moment, ALICE BERRY, *fifty-four, enters from the hall; she is Harry's girlfriend and she shares the house with him. She stops, looks at Harry for a moment; he is absorbed in thought or in the book or the music, and does not at first see her.*

HARRY *suddenly lets out a large sigh.*

ALICE: Harry?
> (*He turns, startled.*)
> How's the – headache? I'm sorry, I didn't mean to – . You had a headache. You took some aspirin?
> (*It has taken him this long to realize who has startled him. Finally, he nods and turns back to his book. The Debussy continues.*)
> Tom's here.
> (*No response.*)
> I just picked him up. His bus was even on time, if you can believe that. A miracle!
> (*She tries to smile.*)
> He's very excited. A weekend out of New York . . .

HARRY: (*Without picking his head up from his book:*) Who's Tom?

ALICE: Harry, I told you about – . You said it was – . We talked about – !!

HARRY: (*Over this:*) It's fine, Alice, I just forget who Tom is!
> (*Short pause.*)

ALICE: He's my – . Bill's brother. He was my brother-in-law. So he's my ex – .

HARRY: (*Over the last part of this, turning to Alice:*) He was good to you, wasn't he? During your divorce. He was very helpful to you.

ALICE: He was, Harry. If you didn't want – .

HARRY: I think that is wonderful! That Tom's here. Someone
   you like. Someone who has been – helpful.
ALICE: I hadn't seen him for – .
HARRY: (*Over this:*) Someone like that doesn't change. Someone –
   helpful. Good.
   (*He turns back to his desk. She looks at him, confused. He pushes
   a button on the CD and the Debussy begins again. Alice turns to
   leave and there in the door, having just arrived, is* TOM BERRY,
   forty. ALICE *is startled.*)
TOM: (*Smiling:*) Sorry. I couldn't find the – . In the bathroom –
   which towels should I . . . ?
ALICE: Tom – this is Harry.
   (TOM *goes to* HARRY *with his hand out to shake.*) '
TOM: How do you do? I can't thank you enough for – . Sometimes
   the city – . It gets so depressing. Most times! (*He laughs.*)
HARRY: (*At the same time, shaking hands:*) Welcome, to our
   humble – . Alice has told me all about you – . She's been
   looking forward to – .
ALICE: (*Over this:*) Tom said the bus ride up – .
TOM: It was beautiful!
HARRY: It's supposed to be a nice weekend. Weather-wise.
ALICE: I heard it might rain, but – .
TOM: Whatever. It's – great to be in the country.
   (*He smiles. No one knows what to say.*)
ALICE: (*Finally:*) I'll show you where we keep the towels, so if
   you need . . .
TOM: (*To* HARRY:) Thank you for inviting me. I'll see you later.
   (ALICE *and* TOM *leave. Pause.*
   HARRY *pushes the button on the CD player and the Debussy
   begins again.*
   He opens the drawer of the desk and takes out a revolver.
   *Without hesitation he cocks it, sets it on the desk, takes off his
   glasses. As he does he notices that they are dirty. With a
   handkerchief he begins to clean them, then realizes what he is
   doing, laughs to himself and stops. He puts down the glasses,
   picks up the gun and puts the barrel to his head.*
   ALICE *enters from the hallway.*)
ALICE: (*Entering:*) Tom's so happy to be – .

2

(She sees what HARRY *is doing.)*
(Screams:) Nooooooo!!!!!!!!!!!
(He pulls the trigger. Gunshot. And he is dead.)

SCENE 2

Much later that evening.
Part of the kitchen of the house. There is a large rustic wooden table,
which has been used both for eating and as a sort of desk. Piles of
papers, bills, catalogues, etc.; a phone, whose cord extends to the wall,
making a kind of obstacle for anyone going around the table. There is
a transistor radio on the table.
The Debussy continues from the last scene, though over the theatre's
speakers now.
TOM *enters from the pantry; he carries a bowl, a spoon, a box of*
cereal. He does not hear the music. He sets his things down on the table
and goes off again. From off, we hear the opening and closing of a
refrigerator. TOM *returns with a carton of milk. He sits, pours the*
cereal, the milk, he reaches across the table for the sugar. He spoons on
the sugar and begins to eat. He stops and turns on the transistor radio.
The Debussy is gone and from the radio we first hear: a pop tune with
a lot of static. TOM *fiddles with the nob; tries another station, then*
another. He hits upon a religious programme. He listens for a moment
to the minister on the programme as he eats.
The phone rings. TOM *doesn't know what to do. He looks in the*
direction of the door. It rings again. And again. He puts down his
spoon, begins to reach for the phone, when the ring stops – someone has
picked up the phone on another extension.
TOM *changes the channel again, then again, then again – everything is*
junk: pop tunes, commercials. After about the twelfth station, he turns
off the radio.
In silence he eats.
ALICE *enters from the living-room; she has a drink in her hand. At first*
she says nothing; TOM *just eats. Then finally:*
ALICE: That was Elizabeth on the phone. She'll be here in a
    minute. She's just down the road at the gas station. She
    couldn't remember the turnoff.

3

TOM: (*Eating:*) Which one is – ?

ALICE: She's the middle child. She lives in the city too. (*She smiles.*) She's in publishing.

TOM: In the same – ?

ALICE: She's with a different house. (*For the first time she notices that he is eating.*)

TOM: I found some cereal, I hope that wasn't – .

ALICE: You haven't eaten anything have you?

TOM: I didn't expect – .

ALICE: You come out for the weekend and – and you don't even get fed! What could I have been thinking – .

TOM: Alice, I'm – .

ALICE: (*Looking for food:*) I'm not normally like –

TOM: I am fine, Alice! Please.

> (*Beat. She stops looking around.*)

I don't expect anything. Not now.

> (*Pause.* TOM *eats.* ALICE *sips her drink.*)

ALICE: You want a drink? I . . .

TOM: If I do, I'll find it.

> (*Neither knows what to say.* ALICE *sighs.*)

ALICE: I've been in his study – cleaning up.

TOM: I thought that's what that woman – .

ALICE: (*Over this:*) She missed some places.

Look at this. (*She holds out the small photo album she's been carrying.*) They're already in the album. I didn't even know he'd got the photos back yet. And they're already in his . . .

TOM: And that is unlike him?

ALICE: Very. (*Looks at the photos.*) From Bermuda. We were there in – . Last month.

> (*Pause. They look at the photos and say nothing.*)

ALICE: (*Hearing something:*) Was that a car? (*Listens.*) No.

TOM: It looks like you had a really nice time.

ALICE: (*Not hearing him:*) He's got papers . . . It'll take weeks to go through everything. I thought the priority seemed to be the cleaning. I didn't think his family should see – . (*To herself, running through a list:*) I called the school. I did that.

TOM: What school?

ALICE: Harry teaches at Dutchess – . I didn't tell you this?

TOM: Maybe you did.

ALICE: (*Over this:*) How could I not tell you this?! What could I have been thinking?!

TOM: Alice!

ALICE: *You're* staying, right?

TOM: If that's what you want.

ALICE: (*Sighs:*) I can't face his family.

TOM: (*taking her hand:*) If I'm not in the way. (*He pats her hand. ALICE, not listening to TOM, turns again toward the door, as if hearing something.*)

ALICE: She doesn't like me. We've only met five, six times – . Harry kept us apart. I asked him to. She's also in publishing.

TOM: So you said.

ALICE: So we know a lot of the same people. (*Hearing TOM:*) Did I?

(*Beat.*)

She's going to walk into here and start telling us all what to do. In my own home. There's her car.

(*Sound of car in the driveway.*)

I think I've done everything. I like that man at the funeral home. I thought funeral home people were supposed to be – . I don't know.

TOM: I guess not all of them are. There are exceptions.

ALICE: (*Smiles:*) And he is one.

TOM: I guess so.

ALICE: So – we're lucky. (*Sighs:*) I feel like I haven't stopped.

TOM: You haven't.

(*ELIZABETH BAKER enters. She is one of Harry's three children. She is thirty-seven.*)

ELIZABETH: Alice!

ALICE: Elizabeth!

(*They hug.*)

ELIZABETH: I don't know what to say. I don't know what to say.

(*ALICE begins to cry; ELIZABETH hugs her. TOM tries to be inconspicuous.*)

ALICE: (*Crying:*) So – you couldn't remember the turnoff.

ELIZABETH: I knew it was – . I should have just followed my instinct. Anyway.

5

(ALICE *gets ahold of herself and they part.* ELIZABETH *looks at* TOM; ALICE *sees this.*)

ALICE: This is Tom. Berry. He was my ex-husband's brother.

TOM: I still am. (*He tries to laugh.*)

ALICE: Right. That's true.

TOM: I always liked Alice. And when she left my brother I liked her even more. (*He smiles at his joke; no one else does.*)
(*To* ELIZABETH:) How do you do?

ALICE: (*To* ELIZABETH:) Do you want something to eat? To drink?

ELIZABETH: (*Shakes her head:*) There was no traffic.

ALICE: It's late.

ELIZABETH: That's why then. (*She looks at* TOM *again.*)

TOM: I came up on the bus. This afternoon. I also live in the city.

ELIZABETH: (To ALICE:) This afternoon? I thought, it only happened – .

ALICE: It did. I called you right away, Liz. Tom – happened to be here for the weekend.
(*Beat.*)

TOM: I needed to get out of the city and Alice was nice enough to . . .
(*Pause.*)

ELIZABETH: Do you have a coke or something?

ALICE: I have some seltzer.

ELIZABETH: Seltzer's fine.
(ALICE *hurries off into the pantry.* TOM *and* ELIZABETH *are left alone.*
Short pause.)

TOM: I'm sorry about your – .

ELIZABETH: (*Interrupting:*) I have a bag in the car. Excuse me.

TOM: Let me – .

ELIZABETH: It's not heavy, please. (*She goes out.*)
(*Alone,* TOM *doesn't know what to do, he sits again, begins to take another bite of cereal, notices the photo album open on the table and begins to look at the open page.*)

ALICE: (*Entering with the seltzer and a glass:*) Where's – ?

TOM: She's getting her bag.

(ALICE *sees that* TOM *has been looking at the album and she goes and looks over his shoulder.*)

ALICE: (*Pointing to a photo:*) Harry bought that bathing suit for me in Hamilton. That was so unlike him. He was scared to buy me anything. Afraid, he said, I'd just take it back. (*She smiles.*) It took me about two days to get the nerve to wear it in public. Finally – I did. (*Short pause.*) After your brother – .
(TOM *looks at her.*)
I'd convinced myself I'd never meet another man. You see other women, my age and – . You see yourself in their shoes. I expected nothing. Then I met Harry.
(ELIZABETH *enters with her bag. Pause. For a moment no one knows what to say. Finally:*)

ALICE: Here's your seltzer.
(ELIZABETH *finally takes it and drinks it.*)

ELIZABETH: (*As she drinks:*) I had lunch with Dick Riley last week. Your name came up, Alice. He said you were the best managing editor they'd ever had. (*Finishes drinking.*) What a shame it was when you left.
(*Beat.*)
So – know that even after a couple of years, you're still missed.

ALICE: (*To* TOM:) I was cheap. I didn't know any better. That's all he means. (*Turns to* ELIZABETH.) The man at the funeral home – he's not bad. He's not what you'd expect.

ELIZABETH: Good.
(*Beat.*)

ALICE: Gemma and Alfred have made it as far as Denver. They have to wait 'til morning for the next flight. They called.

ELIZABETH: Good.
(*Beat.*)
I mean good that they called, not that they have to wait – .

ALICE: I understood. And Paul and Sophie – they'll get a flight in the morning as well. (*Turns to* TOM:) From L.A.

TOM: (*To* ELIZABETH:) I was amazed when she told me everyone lives in the States.

ELIZABETH: Why?

TOM: That's rare, isn't it?

7

ELIZABETH: (*To* ALICE:) He wouldn't say that if he worked in publishing – .

ALICE: (*Over this:*) You wouldn't.

ELIZABETH: (*To* ALICE:) Have you worked out where everyone will sleep? It isn't a very big house.

TOM: I can move – .

ALICE: (*To* TOM:) There's the pullout couch – .

TOM: The floor is fine – .

ALICE: I meant for Paul and Sophie – .

ELIZABETH: (*Picking up her suitcase:*) Let's figure it all out.

ALICE: I think I have. Harry's brother can have my room. It'll work out. I'm going to the grocery store in the morning – .

ELIZABETH: You're not going to cook! There are too many people! I won't let you, Alice. Gemma and I can share a bed. We shared a room as kids.

ALICE: That's what I thought.

ELIZABETH: What about Chinese?

ALICE: There's a terrific Chinese – . Just in our village. Harry loves their dumplings. (*She stops. Corrects:*) He loved them.
(*Short pause.*
ALICE *tries not to cry; she turns to* ELIZABETH:)
He did it in front of me. I think that's what I can't forgive him for.
(*Beat.*)
But I don't think he meant to hurt me.

ELIZABETH: No – .

ALICE: Because, he loved me. (*She takes* ELIZABETH's *hand:*) Your Father was a very – tired man.

ELIZABETH: I know. And he'd been tired for years – long before he'd met you, Alice.

ALICE: (*Looks up at her:*) Thank you.
(*Beat.*)

ELIZABETH: This isn't a surprise. (*Then, to change the subject:*) So – it's Chinese! (*Turns to* TOM:) Do you like Chinese?

TOM: Anything is fine with – .

ELIZABETH: (*Not listening to him, turning to Alice:*) I knew I'd have at least one good idea. I think Father once even mentioned the restaurant – .

8

ALICE: Usually the Chinese food you get up here in the sticks, but this place – .

ELIZABETH: I know what you mean. But I'll bet this place is great. Father always had good taste.

(ALICE *takes* ELIZABETH's *hand.*)

ALICE: Thank you.

(ELIZABETH *realizes that* ALICE *has taken this as a compliment.*)

ELIZABETH: I didn't mean . . . But – of course that too. With you too. That's obvious. Father had impeccable taste.

ALICE: He was a refined and cultured man.

ELIZABETH: I always thought so. Come on. (*She helps* ALICE *up.*) Let's you and I figure out where to put everyone.

(*They go. Pause.* TOM *is alone. He takes another spoonful of cereal and –*)

SCENE 3

The same. The kitchen, early evening of the next day.
[*Note: a few hours ago, Paul (the son) and his wife, Sophie, arrived by rental car from Kennedy Airport. Just a few minutes ago, Gemma (the oldest daughter) and Alfred (Harry's brother) arrived also by rental car from the same airport.*]
PAUL, *32, sits at the kitchen table, surrounded by his two sisters,*
GEMMA, *39, and* ELIZABETH. ALICE *is taking silverware out of a drawer in the table, to set the table for dinner. As the scene begins,*
TOM *has just entered with bags of Chinese food.*

PAUL: (*To* GEMMA:) If we'd known you were arriving at Kennedy – .

GEMMA: (*Over this:*) We didn't know ourselves. We had tickets to Bradley – .

PAUL: (*Over this:*) We'd have waited.

ELIZABETH: (*Over this:*) You could have shared the car rental.

PAUL: Still it'll be useful to have another car up here.

GEMMA: The drive was wonderful. Very relaxing.

PAUL: (*Over the end of this:*) This is my first autumn in three years. You forget what it's like.

9

ALICE: (*Over this:*) Someone said it was supposed to rain.

GEMMA: How's L.A.?

PAUL: Warm and sunny.

ALICE: (*to* GEMMA:) And Albuquerque?

GEMMA: Sunny and warm!

(*They laugh.*)

TOM: (*Who has been holding up the Chinese food, trying to get someone's attention:*) I have the . . . !

ALICE: Let me help, Tom. That was quick. We're all here! Alfred and Gemma just arrived – .

GEMMA: (*To* ELIZABETH, *over this:*) I love New England. You're lucky to be so close.

(*The phone rings.*)

ALICE: (*Same time:*) Excuse me. (*She goes to pick up the phone.*)

ELIZABETH: (*Same time, to* GEMMA:) I never get up here. Father had me up twice, maybe three times. I hardly could remember the way.

ALICE: (*With her hand on the receiver, as it rings:*) I've told everyone it's the best Chinese I've ever had! Even in the city. And in all places – . (*She picks up the phone.*) Hello?

TOM: (*to the others:*) Actually, the place she sent me to – . It appears to have closed. They'd gone out of business, I suspect.

(*Beat.*)

There was another place. Just down the road. (*Holds up the bag of food.*) There was hardly a wait. I don't know how they cook it so fast.

(*Others look at* TOM.)

ALICE: (*Into the phone:*) Yes. At eleven. Here in the garden. Yes, Harry would have liked that.

(*Beat.*)

Thank you so much. See you tomorrow. (*She hangs up.*)

(*Pause.*)

TOM: I hope it's good. The food! (*Smells a bag.*) It smells good.

ALICE: It's always good at that place. 'Harry's Place' was what we called it. Because Harry . . .

ELIZABETH: (*Getting up:*) We'll need some serving spoons.

ALICE: (*Pointing to the drawer in the table:*) In that drawer, Elizabeth.

GEMMA: (*to* TOM:) We haven't met.

ALICE: This is Tom. He's my – . A relative of mine. Gemma. Harry's eldest.

TOM: How do you do?

(*They shake hands.*)

My sympathies. To all of you.

GEMMA: Uncle Alfred will be down in a – .

ALICE: Harry's brother.

GEMMA: (*To* TOM:) Were you very close to our father?

(*Beat.*)

TOM: Close? To tell the truth, I only just met him – .

ALICE: (*Interrupting:*) Where are we going to eat? There's the dining-room.

ELIZABETH: Won't that be too formal? It's just Chinese – .

GEMMA: And we're a family.

ELIZABETH: The kitchen's fine.

GEMMA: Let's eat here. I always eat in my kitchen.

ELIZABETH: Move a few things out of the way – . (*She begins to pick up the papers on the table.*)

ALICE: Smell how good that smells.

GEMMA: (*Over this:*) We'll need large bowls or do we just serve it out of the boxes? At home I just serve it out of the boxes.

ELIZABETH: (*To* ALICE, *over this:*) Is it okay if I just pile these papers together?

PAUL: (*Interrupting:*) Sophie's still taking a nap! Shouldn't we wait for her?

(*Beat.*)

GEMMA: (*To* ELIZABETH:) I forgot she was here. I hadn't seen her so – .

ELIZABETH: She's taking a nap.

PAUL: I just think she might feel – . I don't know – to come down and find us all eating dinner . . .

(*Beat.*)

ELIZABETH: Couldn't you wake her up, Paul? I wouldn't want people waiting to eat because of me.

GEMMA: The food'll get cold.

PAUL: She didn't sleep at all last night. Or on the plane.

(*Beat.*)

ELIZABETH: We can reheat it for her later then.

ALICE: Maybe she's reading, I'll go and see if – . (*Starts to go.*)

PAUL: Let her sleep! Please. I want her to get some sleep.
(*Beat.*)

GEMMA: So we're to – what? The food's here. This makes no
sense.

PAUL: I told her we wouldn't be eating for a while. That's what
Alice told me – .

ALICE: Because I thought there'd be a wait – .

TOM: There wasn't any wait at the restaurant.

ALICE: On a Saturday night?! That's incredible. It's such a
popular place.
(*Short pause.*)

GEMMA: So what are we going to – ?

ELIZABETH: (*Over this:*) What if we don't sit down? What if we
– say, put out the food and whenever anyone wants to – .
Buffet-style. So no one's missing anything. How's that,
Paul? We can keep reheating it, so it's always ready.

GEMMA: Sophie can't get upset about that.

PAUL: It wasn't because she'd get upset – .

GEMMA: I mean, it sounds fair.

PAUL: (*Continuing:*) She's not the one upset, I am. I told her – .
She doesn't care. Why should she care? Whatever we want
to do is fine with – .

ELIZABETH: Fine! Then we'll need some plates – .

ALICE: I'll get them.

PAUL: How would you feel if you walked in on – . And there
was your husband surrounded by his sisters, having dinner
and you'd been told – .

ELIZABETH: We understand, Paul. Forget it.
(ALICE *starts to leave, stops, notices the drink in her hand.*)

ALICE: Who else wants a drink? I forgot to ask. I'll open one of
Harry's good bottles of wine. I think he'd have liked that.
(*Beat.*)

GEMMA: (*After looking at her brother and sister:*) I don't think any
of us drink.
(*The others shake their heads.*)
I suppose we'd seen enough of what that can do – growing

up. But please . . . Don't let us stop you, Alice.
(*Beat.*)

ALICE: Tom? What about you?

TOM: A – . Small glass. Very small.

ALICE: (*To herself as she leaves:*) More for me. (*She goes.*)
(*Pause.* TOM *begins to take the food out of the bags.*
ELIZABETH *and* GEMMA *straighten up the table.*)

GEMMA: (*To* PAUL:) You were right to stick up for your wife.

PAUL: I wasn't sticking up for – .

GEMMA: That was a good thing to do, Paul.
(*Short pause. They continue to get the table straightened.*)

GEMMA: (*To* ELIZABETH:) Where's the body?

PAUL: Gemma, please!

GEMMA: Don't stop us from talking!

ELIZABETH: Some funeral home. Alice says he ought to be
cremated.

PAUL: Oh God.

ELIZABETH: What do you think?

GEMMA: What did father want?

PAUL: Does it matter?

ELIZABETH: Alice has this idea which – . I don't know, it's not
what I'd have expected from her. She seems so – matter-of-
fact. That's her reputation in the city – very matter-of-fact.
(*She looks at* TOM, *who smiles.*)

TOM: I'll find some glasses. (*He goes.*)

ELIZABETH: Alice has this idea in her head about standing in the
garden and throwing his ashes into the air.

GEMMA: That's what she meant on the phone. Is that legal?

PAUL: What harm could – ?

GEMMA: When mother died, she was buried.

ELIZABETH: I know that. But I do not think father would have
wanted to be buried by mother.

GEMMA: Or vice versa.

ELIZABETH: (*Shrugs*) I don't know that. Do we know that?
(*Short pause.*)
What did you feel when you heard, Gemma?
(*Paul sighs.*)
Ignore him. (*She turns to* GEMMA, *then quickly, suddenly back*

to PAUL *to shut him up:*) I wish to talk to my sister!
(*Short pause.*)

GEMMA: I – was angry. I don't think I have ever been so angry
with anyone – ever.
(*Beat.*)
I'd told Father – if he ever did do it – I'd hate him for the rest
of my life.

ELIZABETH: You were angry, but you weren't shocked? I wasn't
shocked. Was anyone shocked?
(*No one says anything.*
ALICE *enters with the plates;* TOM *is behind her with a bottle of
wine, a bottle of seltzer, glasses and a corkscrew.*
There is silence for a long time. TOM *opens the wine bottle;*
ALICE *sets out the plates. When she finishes:*)

ALICE: Since we're eating in the kitchen, I thought we wouldn't
use our fancy plates. These aren't our good plates. We have
much nicer plates than these.
(*Short pause.*)
Do any of you smoke?
(PAUL, GEMMA *and* ELIZABETH *look incredulously at her at
this question.*)
I didn't think so.
(*She picks up her purse and takes out a pack of cigarettes. She
taps one out, then lights it.*)

GEMMA: Neither did father. He hated smoke.

ALICE: Which is why he made me smoke outside. Even in the
rain. The snow.
(*Beat.*)
But from today – I can smoke where I please. As they say,
every cloud has its silver lining.

ELIZABETH: Oh my God!

ALICE: I'm joking, Elizabeth! That was a joke!
(*Beat.*)
Not the smoking – the silver lining.
(*Beat.*)
I'm terribly sorry if it wasn't funny.
(*She exhales, then takes a sip of her drink – the ice cubes clanking
against the glass. Awkward pause.*)

TOM: I'll just dish out the rice into a bowl – .

ALICE: (*As she exhales:*) Look at that rice. I told you the place was good.

PAUL: I think I heard a creak – . Maybe Sophie's . . . (*He gets up.*) I'll go see if she's awake. I'll tell her we're waiting for her.

GEMMA: I thought we weren't waiting for Sophie.

(ALFRED, *Harry's twin brother, enters.*

TOM *sees him and nearly cries out in shock – irrationally thinking this is Harry's ghost. As he sees him he nearly knocks over the wine bottle; glasses tip over, rice spills. Others cry out:* 'Careful!' 'Watch out!' 'Catch it!' *as they scramble to save the glasses, bottle, etc.*)

ALICE: (*To* ALFRED:) Are you unpacked?

ALFRED: Alice, I feel awful kicking you out of your room – .

ALICE: That's silly. Did you look through Harry's clothes?

ALFRED: I haven't had – .

ALICE: If there's anything that – .

ALFRED: Later, Alice.

ALICE: Of course.

PAUL: (*Explaining the table:*) We're waiting for Sophie. When she's awake – .

ELIZABETH: I thought we were setting out the plates – .

ALFRED: She's in the bathroom. She's using the bathroom.

PAUL: (*To everyone:*) Sophie's in the bathroom.

(TOM *has been staring at* ALFRED; ALFRED *now stares back at him.*)

ALICE: This is Tom. You haven't met him. He was out getting the food when you arrived. (*Introducing:*) Tom – Alfred, Harry's brother. Alfred – Tom. He's a relative of mine. Sort of.

ALFRED: And obviously a good friend of Harry's. Thank you for coming.

PAUL: If Sophie's awake – .

ALFRED: She's in the bathroom.

PAUL: (*Over this:*) Then we can set the table. Go ahead and set the table. We'll eat together at the table. (*He goes out.*)

GEMMA: (*To* ELIZABETH:) What happened to buffet-style?

ALICE: (*Half-whisper to* TOM:) They were twins.

15

TOM: (*Still in some shock:*) When I saw him I thought – .

ALICE: I know. It's odd for me too.

ALFRED: Could I have a glass of that? I haven't had a drink for months.

GEMMA: You had two on the plane.

ALFRED: (*Taking the bottle, ignoring* GEMMA; *to* ALICE:) I've been taking care of myself, Alice.

ALICE: It shows, Alfred.

ELIZABETH: Are we setting the table or not?

ALFRED: Is that the famous Chinese Harry was always going on about?

TOM: I'm not sure it's exactly the same – .

ALFRED: He used to say, Alfred, we have the best Chinese take-out in this hick village than anywhere in New York City, San Francisco, Seattle. You name it. In this village, for Christ sake.

TOM: Actually, I don't think it's from the place he – .

ALFRED: It smells good. Harry always loved food.

TOM: Did he?

ALFRED: Loved it. Talked about nothing else.

ALICE: That's not true, Alfred. He rarely – .

ALFRED: Who cares? Now we can say anything we want about the bastard.

(*Short pause.*

ALFRED *stands at the table; and suddenly he nearly collapses.*
Everyone hurries to him, to grab him, as they do they shout:
'What's wrong?' 'Sit down!' 'Get him some water!' 'Are you all right?' *etc.*)

ALICE: (*With a glass of seltzer:*) Here drink this.

(ALFRED *drinks. He holds up his hands – to show that he will be fine. He drinks some more, then finally:*)

ALFRED: You said – in the study? Down the hall.

(*Beat.*)

That's where it was?

(ALICE *nods.*)

I just looked in. I didn't see anything. Have you been cleaning, Alice?

(*Beat.*)

Get someone in. Do yourself a favour. (*He sips, then:*)
I threw up – in the study. I couldn't get anything to clean it
up with. Sophie was in the bathroom.
(*Beat.*)

GEMMA: We'll clean it up, Uncle Alfred.
(*Pause. No one knows what to say.*)

ALFRED: We're eating in here?

ELIZABETH: Maybe you'd like to get some air. The air on
airplanes – .

ALFRED: I'm hungry. I want to try some of my brother's famous
Chinese take-out.

GEMMA: Give Alfred a plate – .

ELIZABETH: (*At the same time:*) Are we sitting down? I'm
confused.

ALFRED: Pull up some chairs. (*Realizing:*) I'm at the head. I
suppose that is where I should be now.

ELIZABETH: We thought it'd be nicer – less formal in the kitchen.

ALFRED: I don't care where I eat.

ELIZABETH: I like it in here. We were all saying – how relaxed it
is in here. Let's set out plates.
(*PAUL enters with SOPHIE, 41; she is French though has lived in
the States for many years.*)

PAUL: Look who's awake!
(*Everyone greets her:* 'Sophie!' 'How was your nap?' 'Sit
down.' *GEMMA and SOPHIE hug as they have not greeted each
other yet. ALICE points to TOM and says:* 'Tom you've met.'
During this, the phone rings and ALICE picks it up.)

SOPHIE: (*Over this:*) Why are you eating in here when there's such
a lovely dining-room?!

PAUL: She's right. We could eat in the dining-room. It'll be much
nicer there.

ELIZABETH: You agreed that the kitchen – .

SOPHIE: Alfred?

ALFRED: I don't care.

ELIZABETH: We're all set up in – . Gemma?

GEMMA: It is a nice dining-room.

ELIZABETH: It's just so much less formal in here.

PAUL: (*Over this:*) Everyone grab something. I'll take the glasses.

ELIZABETH: I like it in here.

SOPHIE: I didn't mean – . (*To everyone:*) If Elizabeth wants us to eat in the kitchen – .

PAUL: Of course, if Elizabeth insists . . .

ELIZABETH: I'm not insisting.

PAUL: Then Tom, could you bring the rice? You be in charge of the rice.

ELIZABETH: (*Over this:*) It just seems silly. We're already in the kitchen – .

ALICE: (*Putting her hand over the receiver; to the others:*) They want to know – should they send flowers or is there some charity . . . ?
(*Beat.*)

SOPHIE: Flowers are such a waste. Don't you think? They just die.

PAUL: A charity then. Did father have a charity – ?

GEMMA: Maybe the school – .

ALICE: He hated the school.

PAUL: Was there anything he . . . ? (*Looks at the others.*)
I don't know.
(*Beat.*)

GEMMA: Who'd father want to give money to??
(*Pause.*)

ELIZABETH: I think flowers would be nice, myself.

ALICE: Then we'll have them send flowers! (*She returns to the phone, relays that flowers would be fine.*
Everyone is standing, carrying something on their way to the dining-room.)

SOPHIE: (*To PAUL:*) I hope this isn't just because I said – .

PAUL: Of course it isn't. It's just a good idea.

ALFRED: (*To GEMMA:*) What about the study? Who's going to clean – ?

GEMMA: There's probably a sponge under the sink in the bathroom. Don't worry about it.

ELIZABETH: (*To GEMMA:*) Don't you think flowers will be nice?
(ALICE *puts down the phone.*)

ALICE: (*To TOM who is balancing a few things:*) There's a tray in the pantry. (*She calls out to everyone as they head off towards*

18

the dining-room.) Why are we moving? Why can't we stay where we are? (*She gets up and follows them out.*)

SCENE 4

The kitchen, a short time later.

ALICE, TOM, ALFRED, GEMMA, ELIZABETH, PAUL *and* SOPHIE *sit around the table, half-way through their Chinese meal. The papers, phone, etc. have been pushed to one side, giving the table a very cluttered look.*

PAUL: (*As he eats:*) I think we actually like L.A. And I know that sounds crazy.

ALICE: No one's eating the moo-shoo.

GEMMA: I tried it.

PAUL: (*Continuing, over some of this:*) And I don't mean the weather. I like the people. I like my work.

ELIZABETH: Isn't it nicer in here than in that stuffy old dining-room?

ALICE: It's not stuffy.

ELIZABETH: Don't you agree, Sophie?

SOPHIE: I didn't mean it to become a thing. I'm sorry.

ELIZABETH: It hasn't become a – 'thing' as you call it. (*She smiles and eats.*)

TOM: (*To PAUL, changing the subject:*) What work do you – ?

PAUL: I read. I'm a reader.

ALFRED: Is that now a professional position in Los Angeles? (*He laughs.*)

PAUL: For films. I read scripts and . . .

SOPHIE: Tell him.

PAUL: I give my opinions. About how to develop those scripts. (*Beat.*)

ALFRED: (*Sips his drink:*) And what is your opinion?

GEMMA: We've had this conversation before. (*To ALFRED:*) You know what Paul does – .

PAUL: (*Over this:*) Depends upon the script, of course.

ALFRED: I would have thought they'd all be rubbish.

PAUL: Some are and some – .

ALFRED: (*Interrupting:*) I can understand liking the weather. Even some of the people. But even you can't keep a straight face when you talk about their movies – .

PAUL: (*Over this:*) My face's completely straight!

SOPHIE: It is!

ALFRED: My mind would go to mush if I had to – !

SOPHIE: It's a good job! A way to learn the business!

PAUL: (*Over this:*) I'm learning what people want!

ALFRED: (*Yelling back:*) They don't know what people want!

PAUL: And in England they do?!

(*Beat.*)

In London today there aren't three people who know how to make a successful movie. That's my opinion.

(*Short pause. No one knows what to say.*)

SOPHIE: And if Paul hadn't moved to L.A., we never would have met.

(*Short pause, as* PAUL's *family bite their tongues.*)

ELIZABETH: Uncle Alfred, you're here. I wouldn't criticize.

ALFRED: They pay me twice what I got at Hull. Full stop. *I* didn't come for the culture.

TOM: (*To* ALICE, *referring to* ALFRED:) What does he do – ?

ALICE: He teaches English.

(*Short pause.*)

(*To everyone:*) Tom *teaches* – acting.

(*Everyone politely nods or mumbles,* 'Oh really.')

(*To* PAUL:) So he's in the performing arts as well.

TOM: Not in L.A. In New York.

PAUL: For theatre?

TOM: Some.

PAUL: I'd have thought you couldn't make a living from the theatre – .

TOM: Students of mine – they do television, films, plays. I mostly do accents.

(*Beat.*)

For Americans trying to be – (*Shrugs:*) English? As well as the other way around.

ELIZABETH: There's a lot of need for – ?

TOM: I survive.

(*Beat.*)

I do the best I can. It's a living. (*To* PAUL:) I like Los
Angeles too.

GEMMA: For me – New Mexico is paradise. Isn't it, Uncle Alfred?
I sit on my porch, brush in hand and paint and before me – .
I don't even have to put on shoes! Before me is a landscape
that is not only the most extraordinary I've ever seen, but it
also *changes*. Totally, completely remakes itself, I don't
know, five hundred times a day! Because of the light, the
clouds, even the density of the air. I don't mean just
shadows, I mean one minute it's yellow and the next it's
blue! (*She smiles and shakes her head.*) It's so different from
England. Or the Alps or Provence where everything's fixed.
Some mornings what gets me out of bed is the thought that if
I weren't out there to paint it all, it'd be lost for good.
(*Beat.*)

ALFRED: (*To* TOM:) She came to visit and she stayed. Every day, I
blame myself.

GEMMA: An amazingly beautiful place. Even you say that
sometimes. I can't imagine living anywhere else now.

ALICE: (*To* TOM:) Gemma's a painter.

TOM: I'd guessed that.

GEMMA: I've wondered what Turner would have made of it.
Where instead of just a sea or sky or horizon, there was a
landscape that was constantly changing, that was all –
movement.
(*Beat.*)
(*Smiles:*) I try. But I'm not Turner, am I? (*Turns to*
ELIZABETH *who says nothing.*) Elizabeth's bought four of my
paintings. She said she bought them as an investment, but I
think she just wanted to give me some money. (*Laughs to
herself;* ELIZABETH *does not correct her. No one is really eating
the Chinese food, which is awful; so they sort of move it around
in their plates.*)

PAUL: Could you pass me the seltzer?

ALICE: (*At the same time:*) New England's very beautiful as well.

SOPHIE: The drive up – .

PAUL: I haven't seen autumn for years.

GEMMA: (*To* ALICE:) There must be – . You must have all sorts of
	special places where you go. Natural – I don't know, you tell
	me.
ALICE: There's a waterfall that's supposed to be – . I haven't seen
	it. I haven't actually driven around very much. Mostly it's
	just been to and from the city.
PAUL: It's a nice drive.
ALICE: I've wanted to see more, but . . .
	(*Beat.*)
TOM: (*To* ALICE:) How long have you lived here? Maybe you told
	me . . .
ALICE: Harry's had the place for – .
ALFRED: Years and years.
ELIZABETH: (*At the same time:*) Fifteen, twenty years.
ALICE: I moved in two years ago, next month. The six months
	before that, I came up every weekend.
	(*Beat.*)
	(*Smiling:*) First it was – 'come on, Alice, stay over Sunday
	night, take the early bus back.' Then I was taking Fridays
	off. Then I quit my job. Sublet my apartment – then sold it.
	(*Silence. No one has anything to say.*)
ELIZABETH: (*Finally:*) Two years? It was that long ago? I hadn't
	even heard about you until . . . (*To her siblings:*) When did
	Father tell about Alice?
	(*No response.*)
GEMMA: (*To* TOM:) And New York is nice as well.
TOM: (*To* ELIZABETH:) You're in the city – .
ELIZABETH: East Eighty-first.
TOM: I'm on the West Side. A Hundred and Third.
ELIZABETH: It's gotten better there.
TOM: It has.
ELIZABETH: I love New York. I wouldn't want to live anywhere
	else. Nothing closes. You can stay out all night.
	(SOPHIE *sighs, wipes her forehead with her napkin.*)
PAUL: What is it?
SOPHIE: I'm fine, I just – .
PAUL: She's sweating.
GEMMA: Maybe the food, it does taste sort of – .

22

ELIZABETH: I stopped eating it – .

PAUL: She's hot.

SOPHIE: I'll be okay. It feels stuffy in here.

ELIZABETH: It would have been a lot stuffier in the dining-room.

ALICE: The stove is on. We can turn that off; I don't think we
     need to keep reheating the – .

SOPHIE: (*Standing:*) Maybe I'm just tired. Would it be impolite if
     I – . Maybe if I just lie down.
     (*Everyone adds:* 'Of course.' 'Please.' 'Get some rest.'
     'Relax.')

GEMMA: (*Over this:*) It's been an exhausting day for all of us.

SOPHIE: I'll come back down later. Maybe if I read. (*She touches
     her head.*) There's aspirin or something in the bathroom?
     (ALICE *nods.* SOPHIE *turns to go, then turns back:*)
     Paul, can you help me look for the aspirin?

PAUL: (*Standing:*) I'm sure it's in the – .

SOPHIE: Paul. Help me look.
     (*She goes.* PAUL *hesitates, then hurries after her. Short pause.*)

ELIZABETH: The dining-room is stuffier. She always seems sick,
     doesn't she?

GEMMA: I hadn't noticed. Paul's never said – .

ELIZABETH: Every time we're together, she's sick. (*To* TOM:)
     She's nine years older than Paul. And I say that to flatter her
     – she looks great. When she's not sick.
     (*Beat.*)
     She's even older than Gemma.

ALICE: Is anyone going to eat anymore . . . ?
     (*No response.*)

ALFRED: How long has she been away from France? I don't think
     I know that.

ELIZABETH: Sophie hasn't lived anywhere but West Hollywood
     since she was eight. She puts that accent on.

TOM: It's a good accent.

ELIZABETH: Remember her mother? We met her at their
     wedding last December – she now sounds like she comes
     from Texas.

ALFRED: Isn't that where she lives – ?

ELIZABETH: Sophie's no more French any more than I am!

ALICE: Maybe she puts the accent on to please Paul.
   (*Beat.*)
ELIZABETH: How do you mean?
   (ALICE *says nothing;* ELIZABETH *considers this, then:*)
   I'll bet your right. (*And she laughs at the thought.*)
ALFRED: She's a nice girl.
TOM: (*Changing the subject:*) Funny, isn't it, all of us – we're living all over *America*. What does that say?
ALFRED: What?
TOM: It's strange. How did it happen? How did *you* – ?
ELIZABETH: I think we all came for different reasons.
ALFRED: Harry was first. He led us all here. Blame him! (*Laughs.*)
ELIZABETH: (*Continuing:*) You can't generalize, I think. For me, London had become so . . . (*Makes a face.*)
GEMMA: (*Over this:*) I followed Alfred. He kept sending postcards of the desert.
ALICE: (*Half over this:*) I was brought over years ago by my publishing company.
   (*This question has definitely animated the table – they talk almost at the same time:*)
ALFRED: (*Continuing:*) Harry left about – twenty years ago was it?
GEMMA: We were kids.
ELIZABETH: I was seventeen. Exactly.
GEMMA: (*To* TOM:) What about you? You asked the question.
TOM: I was offered a job. As a stage manager. I started as a stage manager. I guess you're right, we shouldn't generalize.
ALICE: (*Over this:*) And as for why Harry – Harry's wife, right? She'd just died. Their mother.
   (*Everyone is now listening to this.*)
   You children were all in schools. He wanted to . . . (*Shrugs.*)
   Get away from some memories, I suppose. Clear his head. That's how I've always . . .
   (*Beat.*)
   He didn't plan on staying. I don't know how many times he told me that.
ALFRED: His wife died? Twenty years ago?
ALICE: You must have known that.
   (ALFRED *looks at his nieces.*)

24

He came for – ? I don't know. A semester. That's all he said
he was hired for. Then one thing led to another. And he
stayed.
(*Beat.*)
And one by one – you came.
(*Beat.*)
What's wrong?

ELIZABETH: Mother died – two months ago.
(*Pause.*)

ALICE: What do you mean?

ELIZABETH: We were all at the funeral. Father was there.
(*Beat.*)
He said you'd felt it wasn't appropriate for you to come. We
understood, didn't we?
(*She looks to* GEMMA *who nods.*)

ALICE: Two months ago? Where was the – ?

GEMMA: Brighton. Where mother lived.

ALICE: Harry was in England two months ago?? (*Then suddenly:*)
Oh that's right. Now I remember. Yes, I couldn't come. I
hope Harry sent my condolences. I think I sent flowers.
(*Pause.* PAUL *enters.*)

PAUL: A delicate flower! That is what I tell her she is. Sorry.
Sophie'll be fine; she's tucked in, reading a magazine.
(*Noticing the faces:*) What's . . . ?

ALFRED: We were telling Tom how Harry came to the States.

PAUL: You've told him that Mother just threw him out?

ALICE: Did she?

PAUL: She'd had enough of him. She used to say that marrying
Father was like buying a boat; your happiest times are when you
get it, and when you get rid of it. (*He laughs, no one else does.*)

ALICE: What exactly had your father done for your mother to
throw him out?
(*Beat.*)

ELIZABETH: (*After checking with her siblings:*) She never said. I
don't think we ever asked.

GEMMA: There's a lot we don't know. Why didn't they ever
divorce – . (GEMMA *is about to continue a list.*)

ALICE: (*Interrupting:*) Harry was still married to your mother?

25

GEMMA: Didn't you know that?
>   (*Pause.*)
TOM: (To PAUL:) So your wife is just tired.
ELIZABETH: She looked tired.
TOM: I gather you've only been married – .
PAUL: Not even a year. It's made a big difference in my life.
TOM: Something like – .
ALICE: (*Standing:*) Excuse me. (*She takes the bottle of wine and fills up* ALFRED'*s glass.*) I should get more.
TOM: I can go if – .
ALICE: I know where Harry's best stuff is hidden. (*She goes.*)
>   (*Beat.*)
ELIZABETH: Father never told her he was still married.
GEMMA: (*Picking up plates:*) Is anyone still eating?
TOM: (*Taking a last bite:*) I've had a lot worse in New York.
ELIZABETH: Father didn't tell her. What does that say?
ALFRED: Harry once talked to me – about Alice.
>   (*Beat.*)
ELIZABETH: And . . . ?
ALFRED: He said he'd met this woman. Alice. And, I think he said, that their relationship was – the word he used was – 'comfortable.' (*He looks to* TOM.)
TOM: She's a nice woman. I'm not going to say anything to her that could hurt her.
ELIZABETH: 'Comfortable.'
>   (*Beat.*)
>   What are we going to do about this cremating-idea? Alice said she thought that's what Harry would have – .
PAUL: Alice said.
>   (*Beat.*)
GEMMA: Do we know what Father – .
PAUL: Mother was buried.
GEMMA: And he certainly would not have wanted to be buried with – .
PAUL: Do we know that for sure?!!
>   (*Beat.*
>   *Phone rings. In the middle of the second ring, it stops. Someone else in the house has picked it up.*)

26

I'm still hungry. Maybe there's some peanut butter or something.

ELIZABETH: What are we going to do? Don't you think it's a mistake? I think we tell Alice that we want our father buried. If she gives us any flack we tell her that's what he'd told us he wanted.

GEMMA: We should tell her now.

PAUL: What about the service tomorrow in the garden – .

ELIZABETH: We'll make it a memorial. People can still come, whatever.

(*Beat.*)

Is it agreed?

(*The others nod.*)

Then we'll tell her.

ALFRED: (*Turns to* TOM:) How well *did* you know my brother?

TOM: I didn't know him at – .

ALFRED: I think that's how most of his friends felt. Let me tell you the truth. Harry wasn't a very nice man. He wasn't very nice to me and I wasn't alone. And I got a job at the University of New Mexico and he was working in a bloody community college! And he said this country would eat me alive! (*He laughs.*) You know what they say about twins? That there's always a good one and a bad one.

TOM: I can't believe that's – .

ALFRED: Guess which he was.

(*Beat.*)

Go ahead and guess.

(*Beat.*)

TOM: The bad one?

ALFRED: You knew him well! Still, I think his friends – like yourself – were too hard on him. He used to say that to me. He had a lot of sides to him – Harry. Be fair, Tom. Don't be too quick to judge.

TOM: (*Confused:*) I wasn't – .

ALFRED: Give the man the benefit of the doubt, for Christ sake.

(ALICE *enters with a bottle of wine. The others look to* ELIZABETH *to begin a conversation, but before she can begin:*)

ALICE: (*Opening the wine:*) That was the funeral home – we can pick up the ashes anytime now.

(*She pours herself a glass of wine, sits down and opens the photograph album. No one says anything for a moment, then, holding up the album:*) Our photo album. (*Pointing to a picture:*) Bermuda. (*To* ELIZABETH:) Harry bought me the bathing-suit.

(*Pause. She continues to look. No one knows what to say, when finally:*)

TOM: (*To* PAUL:) Read any good film scripts lately?

ALFRED: (*Almost chokes on his wine, laughing:*) Right!

PAUL: The funny thing about living in America as a foreigner is the way you see other foreigners act. They love to criticize. Everything's – what? Rubbish? Some things are and some things aren't. That's how I see things, but . . . I had a friend from London visiting with us – to him everything was either stupid or plastic or barbaric. Then you couldn't get him out of the damn sun. At night you couldn't get him away from the damn TV. (*He sips his water.*) But I know why this is. I've thought about this a lot. It's all so – threatening. It's too much for some people to handle. The size of everything. The importance of everything. So they're actually being defensive. They're scared.

(*Beat.*)

I hate having friends from home visit now. It's so predictable.

(*To* TOM:) To answer your question: I have read a couple of nice scripts this week. We'll see. I've been reading long enough to know that you can never know. You do your best. And try to have an impact where you can. (*He sips his water.*) The other day, I had a thought. You get these kinds of thoughts reading scripts. Let's say there are maybe ten thousand film scripts in circulation in L.A. on any given day.

ELIZABETH: That many – ?

PAUL: I think I'm being conservative. And each script will have at least twenty copies. Probably more, but let's say twenty. And each script – the rule is about 110 pages. That's – . I did the math before, something like twenty-two million pages of film script just – on any given day.

(*Beat.*)
Now if each writer were to say just indent – both left and right margins – by say three spaces less. Three spaces – no more. It would mean each script would be about five pages shorter – or a total savings of about one million pages, which I'm told roughly equals 200 trees.
(*Short pause.*)
I wrote a memo. (*Shrugs.*) Who knows?
(*Pause.*)
ALICE: I did – know about Harry being married.
(*Short pause. She goes back to looking at the album.*)
ALFRED: (*Looks at* ALICE, *then:*) He talked to me about you, Alice. Harry.
(*She looks up.*)
He said the nicest things. He told me how much he loved you. This new 'gal' he called you. He said – you were everything to him.
(*She nods and goes back to the album.*)
ELIZABETH: (*To* PAUL:) There are so many Brits in publishing here. I have friends – Americans who say the only way to advance is to go first to England – or fake a British accent.
(*She laughs.*)
GEMMA: (*To* TOM:) Work for you!
(*Laughter.*)
TOM: (*Over this:*) So that's why they take my classes!
(*More laughter. Short pause.*)
GEMMA: All of my English friends – such as they are in New Mexico – make fun. It's an easy place to make fun. On the one hand I suppose Paul is right – they're scared. We are. But on the other, you can't help yourself – there's so much that's crazy.
ELIZABETH: Father used to make fun – lest we forget.
PAUL: Father was scared too.
GEMMA: He didn't make fun, he hated. The last time I called him – he just started ranting.
PAUL: About?
GEMMA: He hated this country and everything it tries to be. Or doesn't try to be.

29

PAUL: He loved looking down his nose – .

ELIZABETH: I never took him seriously when he talked like that. It was just talk. I laughed at him, Paul.

PAUL: You encouraged him.

ELIZABETH: He made me laugh, as I've just said. And he wasn't scared, Paul – he was angry.

PAUL: (*Erupts:*) If the man wasn't scared then why the hell are we here?!! And he hated all right! But the only thing he really hated was himself!!

(*Beat.*)

Isn't that now obvious?

(*Pause.*)

ALICE: (*Holding up the album:*) You all might be interested in this. The photos go back years. You're all in here.

ELIZABETH: Pass it around.

ALICE: In a minute, when I'm done. (*She continues to look through the album as she lights a cigarette.*)

ALFRED: I'm all in favour of keeping your sense of humour about things. Sometimes I think it's the only thing of any value that we have left. And if Americans wish to make fools of themselves in front of us – day after day after day after day – what are we supposed to do, cover our eyes? Well I don't. (*Shrugs.*) So shoot me, Paul.

GEMMA: (*To* PAUL:) And I don't know what you're talking about. (*To* ELIZABETH:) Have you heard him do his American accent?

TOM: American accent – ??

PAUL: (*At the same time:*) Once. I did it once!

GEMMA: (*Over this:*) Get off! Let's hear it, Paul!

ELIZABETH: When did he – ?

GEMMA: At his wedding!

PAUL: I only do it in England!

ALFRED: Come on, Paul.

GEMMA: (*Over this:*) Tom here can help you improve it!

(ELIZABETH, GEMMA, ALFRED *and* TOM *are now all shouting to* PAUL *to do his American accent. He is resisting – all in good humour, with a lot of sisterly pushing and nudging.* 'Please, Paul!' 'We want to hear, Paul!' 'I'll bet you can't do one!' *etc.*

As the noise reaches its peak, with people banging on the table and hitting glasses with knives, urging PAUL *to do his 'American' – * SOPHIE *enters in a nightgown and robe.*)

SOPHIE: What's . . . ?

(*They see her and stop. Short pause.*)

I'm sorry, I didn't mean to . . . You were making so much noise, I didn't know what . . . I see – you were just having fun.

(*Beat.*)

Good for you. I'm sure it's not easy to find much to laugh about on a day like today. I'm sorry if I interrupted. (*She turns to go.*)

PAUL: Sophie, sit down if you – .

SOPHIE: (*Interrupting:*) I don't think I'm dressed for a party.

(*Beat.*)

Come up when you feel like it, Paul. When you're ready. I'll wait up.

(*She goes. Pause.*

PAUL *stands, looks at his sisters, then picks up a knife, and says in his best 'Brando' or 'Pacino':*)

PAUL: Hey woman, how come you just don't cut the whole thing off!

(*He turns back to his sisters, smiles and they burst out laughing. Through the laughter they shout:* 'He's good!' 'That was very good.' ALICE *continues to look through the album. As the sisters laugh,* SOPHIE *returns.*)

SOPHIE: Perhaps I will join you. (*She goes and sits next to* PAUL.) I can't sleep anyway. I told Claire I'd call at seven – her time.

GEMMA: How is Claire, you haven't said a word – .

ELIZABETH: (*Over this:*) I meant to ask . . .

SOPHIE: She's very upset, of course. She adored Harry. Even though they'd only met the one time at the wedding. Still, we always put her on the phone when we called. She said, when we told her – of course we didn't say how – she said, 'So how many grandparents do I have now?' (*She smiles.*) She's going to write you each a note.

(*Beat.*)

ELIZABETH: (*To* TOM:) Claire is Sophie's nine-year old – .

31

TOM: I guessed.

SOPHIE: She's devoted to Paul. Worships him, doesn't she?
   (*Beat.*)
   I'm jealous. (*Smiles.*)

GEMMA: (*To* ELIZABETH:) What time is it?

ELIZABETH: Too early to go to bed.
   (*Short pause, then:*)

SCENE 5

The kitchen. An hour or so later.
[ALICE, ALFRED, *and* ELIZABETH *are out for a walk.*]
SOPHIE *sits at the table, talking on the phone to her daughter in
California: what they are saying cannot be heard.* GEMMA *is
beginning to clean up the table, piling dishes, scraping plates, etc. and
carrying them (off) to the sink and garbage.* TOM *and* PAUL *sit across
from each other, talking.*

TOM: (*In the middle of a story:*) 'What are you up for, dear?' I ask.
   (*In American:*) 'It's a play by Oscar Wilder. Do you know
   him?' (*Own voice:*) 'Not for years. Have you done English
   accents before on stage?' (*American:*) 'I was in a show by
   George Bernard Shaw once.' 'Funny, I hadn't realized he'd
   written – shows. And what part did you play?' (*American:*) 'I
   was one of those dancers, you know, in the ballroom scene.'

PAUL: What ballroom – ??

TOM: *My Fair Lady.*

PAUL: Of course!

TOM: (*Over this:*) Last year in her prep school. (*American:*) 'I wore
   the pink dress?' 'I should have guessed just by looking at
   you. What else could you have played?' (*He sips his drink.*)

PAUL: Once – .

TOM: Just a second. (*He continues:*) I reply, after listening to her
   act – I use the term loosely – for a few moments: 'I can see
   there is nothing I can teach you.' (*American:*) 'Oh, but there
   must be!' She had your typical American sense of irony.
   Anyway, to make a long story short, I tried. Her mother paid
   me fifty bucks to go and see her Gwendolen or (*American:*)

'Gwendolen' is how her fellow actors – again the term is used with freedom bordering on abandonment – referred to her character on stage. In the end I would hazard to say she was the most authentic thing in the whole evening.

(*Beat.*)

I met the director after the 'show', which by the way is the appropriate term for what I saw, they, the Americans, have that right – he was, I would say, the most tired human being I have ever been exposed to. He literally fell asleep while *he* was talking to me. But then I'd learned that this was something like the ninth prep-school production of *Importance of Being Ernest* he'd directed in – I think he said – the last three weeks. But maybe I didn't hear him right.

(GEMMA *returns from the sink and picks up more dishes.*)

PAUL: Where in England was he from?

TOM: He was from England, you knew! Bristol, he said. But he may have only been mumbling that in his sleep – a memory? Of something else perhaps?

(SOPHIE *suddenly laughs at something her daughter has told her on the phone.* PAUL *looks at her then back at* TOM, *who pours himself more wine from the bottle.*)

He perked up after a couple of drinks though. His 'Gwendolen's' Mum was paying. Then after we were in this bar for a while, the Mum says (*American:*) 'So what did you really think?' To me. I look at the director, and he says, could I wait a minute, he's really interested in what I have to say, but he has to go to the loo. He gets up, goes – and we never see him again. (*Sips his drink.*) I suppose he had another show to direct. He did say, sometime during the evening, that the highpoint of a busy artistic year was being allowed – by someplace somewhere – to do a production of a Chekhov play. He couldn't recall which one.

(GEMMA *laughs at this.*)

PAUL: My favourite – .

TOM: I haven't quite – .

PAUL: (*At the same time:*) I'm sorry, I didn't mean – .

TOM: (*At the same time:*) But go ahead, please . . .

(*Beat.*)

PAUL: My favourite's . . .

    (GEMMA *stops to listen*.)

    I'm in line at the grocery store. I obviously must have said something, because this fellow behind me, hearing the accent I suppose, says: (*American:*) 'What the fuck is going on with that Queen of yours? Why she letting 'em push her around! If I was Queen I wouldn't let nobody push me around. That lady needs some balls!' (*Smiles*.) They say whatever comes into their heads, I swear. There's no – editing.

    (*Beat*.)

TOM: That's funny. (*Continues with his story:*)

    So – the Mum, she says 'I thought every penny I'd laid out for those lessons was worth it.' (*Looks at* PAUL *and shrugs*.) I suppose I must have done some good. I don't know.

    (*Beat*.)

    I can't work miracles. But sometimes I guess I do okay.

    (PAUL *nods*.)

PAUL: It can be a strange place.

GEMMA: (*As she picks up dishes:*) Sometimes – I pretend, when I'm sitting out on my porch, painting – I look out across the landscape and I say: this is Africa. Like a hundred, hundred and fifty years ago. Africa. (*She starts to leave with the dishes*.) Or India. It makes me feel better for some reason. (*She goes*.)

    (SOPHIE *holds out the phone*.)

SOPHIE: Paul, talk to Claire. I have to get a book to read to her.

PAUL: I'll get it for you – .

SOPHIE: (*Over this:*) It's in my bag. You'll never find it. And besides, Claire's dying to talk to you. (*Into phone:*) Here's Paul, dear. He's grabbing the phone from me, he wants that much to talk to you. (*He obviously has not been grabbing the phone; she now hands it to him. As she does, to* TOM:) I always read to Claire at night. (*She goes*.)

PAUL: (*Into the phone:*) Hi! What did you do today? I'm sure you already have, I'll ask her to tell me. What's the weather like?

    (GEMMA *returns from the sink*.)

TOM: (*To* GEMMA:) I had one student. This was when I'd only been here a few years. My wife couldn't believe this.

GEMMA: (*Interrupting:*) Your wife? I didn't know you were – .

TOM: We're divorced. (*Continues with story:*)
He comes in. His shirt's unbuttoned down to – . And it's goddamn winter. (*Laughs.*)

GEMMA: Was she English?

TOM: My wife? Yes. She's back in London now.
(*Beat.*)
When we were breaking up, I used to say to her: (*in American*) 'What's the matter, can't you take it?' (*He smiles.*) She couldn't.
(*Beat.*)

GEMMA: I didn't mean to be – .

TOM: That's – .

GEMMA: I just suddenly realized. I don't know anything about you. Here you are at . . . . . .

TOM: Alice wanted me to stay – .

GEMMA: I wasn't saying – . Of course you're . . . (*Stops herself.*) Kids?

TOM: Six and nine. Boys. In London.
(*Beat. Then, changing the subject before it becomes too personal:*)

GEMMA: Anyway, you were saying about a student . . .

TOM: He comes into my class, this kid really, and he says to me, in front of everyone, (*American:*) 'I want to try some of that British bullshit acting, you know – with the funny voice.'
(*He laughs, then she laughs, not quite understanding.*)

PAUL: (*Covering the phone:*) I missed that.
(TOM *pours himself more to drink.*)

GEMMA: (*To* PAUL:) A student of Tom's – he wanted to learn the way the British act.
(PAUL *doesn't understand.*)

TOM: Another story! A young woman – she's been a model, now she wants to act. So I've asked her to prepare something. Not that I'm going to reject anyone. God forbid that we have standards.
(PAUL *sets the phone on the table.*)
So she recites: (*American*) 'Thus do I ever make my fool my purse.' I ask her if she knows what she's saying. She says that *for her* it means – how she shouldn't spend so much money

35

on clothes. She says, (*American*) 'That may not be what it means to others, but that's what it means to me.'
(*Beat.*)
I ask her: does she know what character she is acting? She says: (*American*) 'Iago.' Very good. I ask her: did she know that Iago was a – man? She says: (*American*) 'So what? My last drama teacher – .' 'Drama. Drama.' My favourite American word. 'My last drama teacher said there were no male or female parts anymore – only people parts.' I want to say, I think your teacher could have chosen a better word than 'parts', but I bite my tongue. (*Opens his mouth.*) See? Seven years in this country and there's permanent teeth marks there. (*Continues:*) 'Only people parts.' Interesting. Why not? I say to myself, she's paid in advance. Then about a half hour later, for the hell of it or maybe I'm just wanting to get into the swing of this 'people-part' notion, I say, 'Now that you've done your Iago, what about trying Othello?'
(*Beat.*)
You'd have thought I'd hit her in the face. (*Amercan:*) 'Othello,' she says in her lovely American, 'I couldn't do Othello.' 'Why is that, my dear?' 'Othello is a black man.' Or is it 'African-American' now? I don't know and I don't give a fuck. Anyway, 'A black man. And only a black man can play a black man.'
(*Beat.*)
I asked if she felt that was in any way contradictory to what she'd said about 'people-parts'? And she said, she didn't see why it was.
(*Pause.*)
They don't see themselves. They don't question themselves.
PAUL: And the things you can't say. Sometimes I think a decent English comic would be in prison in a wink in this country.
GEMMA: (*Entering from the sink:*) I thought you loved America?
PAUL: You can love something and still find fault with it.
(SOPHIE *enters with the book.*)
SOPHIE: I'd put it in your bag for some reason.
(*She notices the phone on the table.*)
PAUL: We had a nice talk.

(SOPHIE *picks up the phone and begins to read from* Charlie and the Chocolate Factory *to her daughter.*)

TOM: If they weren't so thin-skinned. Sometimes you just want to scream: 'RELAX!'
(*Noise outside.*)

GEMMA: They're back from their walk.

TOM: Anyway, why did you let me go on like that? It must have been very boring, you should have stopped me.
(ALFRED, ALICE *and* ELIZABETH *enter from their walk;* ALICE *and* ALFRED *wear wellingtons.*)

ALICE: What a beautiful night. You should have come with us, Gemma.

PAUL: You've been gone for ages. Where was there to walk? I thought father only had a half acre.

ELIZABETH: We walked through other people's. They don't have fences. (*She looks to* GEMMA *who picks up more plates.*)

GEMMA: I've been picking up.

ELIZABETH: You shouldn't have to do it all.

GEMMA: I was hoping I wouldn't have to.

SOPHIE: (*To everyone:*) Would you mind – ? Please. Sh-sh.
(*She continues to read on the phone.*)

PAUL: Sophie, I don't think you can ask everyone – . It's the kitchen – .

SOPHIE: Fine! I'm sorry I'm in the way.

PAUL: No one said – .

SOPHIE: I'll go upstairs. If it isn't a big bother could someone hang up the receiver when I get to the phone upstairs? (*She goes, carrying her book.*)

ELIZABETH: Is that the same call she was making – ?

ALFRED: (*Sitting taking off his Wellingtons; reads the bottom of the boots:*) (*American*) 'Made with pride in the U.S. of A.' (*To the others:*) Are we still doing our American?

ALICE: (*Over this, to* ELIZABETH:) I'll look for that stomach medicine – .

ELIZABETH: You said it was in the medicine chest. I'm not dumb.

GEMMA: Is something . . . ?

ALFRED: Her stomach.

37

ELIZABETH: (*As she leaves the kitchen:*) And you could help
    Gemma, Paul. You're not home. (*She goes.*)
TOM: (*Standing.*) Let me, I – .
GEMMA: You're a guest.
    (*Turns to* ALICE:) Her stomach?
ALICE: It's the emotion. She holds everything in.
ALFRED: She said it was the Chinese food. I better open another
    bottle. (*Starts to leave for the pantry. American:*) 'What should
    it be? Red or white – or blush?' (*He laughs to himself and
    goes.*)
    (GEMMA *and* PAUL *start to head for the sink, carrying the
    glasses, plates, etc.*)
GEMMA: (*As they go:*) I can't believe Sophie wanted us to be
    quiet – .
PAUL: She didn't mean – . Sometimes she says things without
    thinking. Who doesn't?
    (*They are gone.* ALICE *and* TOM *are alone.* ALICE *suddenly
    sighs.*)
TOM: Are you all – ?
ALICE: It's late.
    (*Beat.*)
    And no one wants to go to sleep.
TOM: Alice – .
    (*She turns to him.*)
    Take care of yourself. This can't be easy.
    (*She smiles, takes his hand and pats it.*)
ALICE: When we were walking – . Elizabeth spent most of the
    time on a bench – . So Alfred . . .
    (*Beat.*)
    He asked me to go to bed with him.
TOM: He's drunk. He's been drinking all – .
ALICE: Thank you.
TOM: I mean – . I meant, don't be too angry with him. Harry's
    death . . . Everyone in this house. You can see how
    emotional it all is.
ALICE: Thank you, again.
TOM: What do you want me to say?
ALICE: 'Do you want to go to bed with him, Alice?'

(*Beat.*)

And the answer to that is . . . (*She shrugs.*)

(*Beat.*)

It was very beautiful out tonight. I love the fall. There was nearly a full moon. Maybe by tomorrow night. I'm going to have a cigarette. I don't give a shit. (*She takes out a cigarette and lights it.*)

GEMMA: (*Off; call:*) My God, Paul's washing a dish!

TOM: Don't do anything that . . . You might regret tomorrow, Alice.

ALICE: What a bullshit thing to say to me!

TOM: (*Over this:*) Then don't ask me for my – !

ALICE: Who asked you?!

(*Beat.*)

Don't worry, I'm not stupid. I'm not going to bed with him. It's nice being asked though.

(ALFRED *enters with the wine. Short pause. He looks at both of them.*)

ALFRED: Did I interrupt something? What were you talking about?

(*Beat.*)

ALICE: Harry. Of course.

(ELIZABETH *enters with the medicine.*)

ELIZABETH: (*Entering:*) None of this kind of stuff ever works for me. I don't know why I'm bothering. Could you hand me a spoon?

(TOM *takes a spoon out of the drawer and hands it to her.*)

GEMMA: (*Off:*) Elizabeth, look what our brother's doing? Have you ever seen him wash a dish in his life?

ELIZABETH: I'll get a camera! (*To the others:*)

Who's paying for that phone call by the way? She's still on the phone. Is she going to read the whole book to her?

ALICE: I assumed it was a credit card call.

ELIZABETH: I think we better ask Paul. (*She goes off to the sink.*)

ALFRED: So you were talking about Harry. There were times when we'd be together, Harry and me, and I'd look at him, sipping his Scotch, and it was like I didn't know that man at all. I had no idea what he was thinking. What he was feeling.

Which is a weird feeling, when the guy looks just like you.

PAUL: (*Entering and heading for the upstairs:*) I'll talk to her. I didn't realize it was bothering everyone!

ELIZABETH: (*Following him in:*) Alice shouldn't be asked to pay – .

PAUL: (*Over this:*) Get off my back!

(*He goes.* GEMMA *also enters from the sink, wiping her hands. Pause.*

ELIZABETH *pours the medicine and drinks it. Finally:*)

GEMMA: You know we've hardly talked about the service.

ALICE: Alfred and I were talking about it on our walk. He was saying he thought Paul wanted – to sing something.

GEMMA: Paul said that?

ALFRED: He hinted to me, when we were – .

ELIZABETH: What does he want to sing?

(*Beat.*)

GEMMA: Father hated Paul's singing. It offended him.

ALICE: Perhaps that is why Paul wants to sing. Maybe each of us – something. Before we throw the ashes into the garden. I was going to read a poem.

TOM: Maybe it's none of my business, but what I would suggest is that you make a list. Put what you're going to do in the order you plan to do it in. You can always change, of course, but . . . It's a good thing to have written down. That's been my experience. In front of people. (*He looks at each one of them.*) I can be secretary if you'd like. If that'd make it easier. Is there a piece of paper?

(*Everyone ignores him. Short pause.*)

ALFRED: (*Sits and leans over and takes* ALICE's *hand:*) I wasn't lying. He told me that he loved you.

ALICE: I know he did.

(*Beat.*)

ALFRED: (*To everyone:*) I noticed a pile of jigsaws in the closet. Anyone else like to do jigsaws? I'll choose one. (*He goes.*)

(*No one has anything to say.* ELIZABETH *turns on the radio for a moment – pop music – she turns it right off again.* ALFRED *enters with a puzzle.*)

ALFRED: (*Holding up the front of the box:*) The Grand Canyon!

40

(ELIZABETH *suddenly grabs stomach in pain, and cries out.*)

GEMMA: Elizabeth!

(GEMMA *and* ALICE *go to her, as she doubles over and nearly collapses to the floor.*)

ALICE: Oh my God!

ELIZABETH: I'll be fine. Give me some water. I'm fine.

(ALICE *gives her some water.* ELIZABETH *sits back in her chair, breathing heavily now. She wipes the sweat from her brow.*)

ELIZABETH: (*Faintly:*) Do the jigsaw. I like jigsaws.

(ALFRED *opens the box and pours out the pieces onto the table.* PAUL *storms into the kitchen from upstairs. He is very upset.*)

PAUL: (*Entering:*) I'll pay for the goddamn call!!! What do you want – a check?! Cash?!!! Whatever you want!! Just get off my back!! She's trying to talk to her daughter!! Is that so bad?! Can't you leave her alone?!!! She's up there crying now. She thinks you hate her! I can't stand it anymore!! Grow up!!!

(*He suddenly becomes aware that* SOPHIE *is behind him. She has been crying.*)

SOPHIE: Paul, your sisters meant well. You shouldn't talk to them like that.

(*Beat.*)

Apologize.

(*Beat.*)

You heard me. Apologize.

(*Beat.*)

PAUL: I'm sorry.

(SOPHIE *tries to smile.*)

SOPHIE: I'm going to bed now – everyone. Goodnight.

(*Everyone except* PAUL *says 'Goodnight' or 'Goodnight, Sophie.'* SOPHIE *turns to go, then turns back:*)

Paul, stay up as late as you want. And visit. (*She leaves.*)

ALFRED: (*Over the puzzle:*) Anyone else ever been to the Grand Canyon? I know you have Gemma. Elizabeth?

(*She nods. He looks at the others, and one by one they nod as well.*)

Everyone?

GEMMA: (*To* ELIZABETH:) You should go to bed. I'll take you up. Come on. (*She helps* ELIZABETH *up*.)

Goodnight. Say goodnight.

ELIZABETH: (*to the others:*) Goodnight.

(*Others say:* 'Goodnight.')

ALICE: Sleep well.

GEMMA: I'll come back down and help.

(*They go*.)

PAUL: I'll finish with the dishes.

TOM: Why can't I – .

PAUL: I'm used to it. It's my job at home. (*He goes to the sink*.)

(TOM *now sits between* ALFRED *and* ALICE. ALFRED *continues to work on the puzzle – turning over pieces, occasionally matching two. He continues this throughout the rest of the scene.* TOM *begins to feel a little uncomfortable between these two*.)

ALICE: About a year ago, Alfred – . (*She ignores* TOM.) Harry started going on and on about this new student of his. A young woman. Said she was – . Amazing. I ran into the two of them one afternoon in the parking lot of the college, chatting. She's beautiful.

(*Beat*.)

You may see her here tomorrow. I think she's invited herself.

(*Beat*.)

After seeing her, I said to Harry, what the hell did he take me for? I didn't want any of that. My last husband – . (*She turns to* TOM *and pats his hand*.) Tom's brother. (*She turns back to* ALFRED.) I'd had it with that. I can live alone. I don't mind.

(*Beat*.)

He smiled – the way he smiled. The way you smile. He was a handsome man.

(ALFRED *looks up*.)

And he kissed me on the lips or tried to. And he said, I don't believe what I'm hearing, Alice. That girl is probably the best violin student I've ever had in America. Her potential is limitless. Finally I feel my talents as a teacher can be fulfilled. You can't know how lucky I feel. Though.

42

of course I'm trying to convince her to transfer to Julliard. (*Beat.*)

I felt like shit. (*She looks at* TOM, *then back at* ALFRED.) He spent a lot of time with her. He loved teaching. (*Short pause.*)

Then one day, I happened by his office door. It was opened a crack. There's also a little window. And there she was with him. She had her violin. I saw her put it under her chin. Raise her bow. And I don't know what I was prepared for, Alfred, but – she was the worst violinist I have ever heard. (*She smiles without looking up.*) I mean it was painful. (*Beat.*)

He screwed around all the time. Though after hearing the girl play I realized that there was some suffering on his part as well. It wasn't all . . . (*Shrugs.*)

Maybe even more suffering than pleasure. (*She smiles.*) We can hope.

(*Short pause. She reaches over and takes* ALFRED'S *drink and takes a sip.*)

So – a few months ago Harry was in England? At his – wife's funeral? What did she die of? Do we know? (*Beat.*)

ALFRED: Her liver. She was a drinker.

(ALICE *takes another sip of* ALFRED'S *drink.*)

ALICE: It was a nice walk. Harry never wanted to take a walk with me after supper. Except – when we were courting. For that one week – he would. (*She looks at* ALFRED. *He looks up. They look into each other's eyes.* TOM *turns away and tries to be invisible.*)

SCENE 6

The kitchen. One o'clock in the morning.
TOM *and* PAUL *sit at the table, working on the puzzle – the frame is now completed. From above, there is a banging/pounding sound.*

(*Beat.*)

43

PAUL: (*Looking up, after listening for a moment:*) Unbelievable. Don't you find it – ? (*Stops himself.*) What were we talking about?

TOM: (*without looking up from the puzzle; American accent:*) 'What you don't understand . . . '

PAUL: (*Remembering where he was; American:*) 'What you don't understand about America is . . . ' Fill in the blank. I don't know how many times I have been told that. 'You don't understand – ' that there was – 'all these different races.' That America is – 'soooo big.' That 'we actually vote for our leaders.'

(*More banging from above interrupts him. He stops.* GEMMA *enters from the sink and stove area; she has just made herself a cup of tea. She wears a nightgown and a robe.*)

GEMMA: (*Listening to the noise above:*) I hope to God I have Uncle Alfred's genes.

PAUL: It's been going on for like an hour now.

(*Beat.*)

Am I the only one offended by this? By our – recently deceased father's girlfriend and our recently deceased father's brother screwing like a couple of bloody rabbits up there in his own goddamn bedroom?!! (*Looks at* GEMMA *who sips her tea.*) No one else is even a little troubled by this turn of events? No? Fine. Then it must be me. (*Turns to* TOM:) What were we talking about? I keep forgetting.

TOM: I heard this once: (*American*) 'I love England. It's my favourite of those countries.'

(*Beat.*)

I should have said – by 'those countries' do you happen to mean *Europe*? Europe the home for the past three millennia to what we humbly call – Western Civilization?!! (*He smiles and shakes his head.*)

GEMMA: Don't you two get tired of complaining?

(*More banging upstairs.* GEMMA *sits down at the table and picks up a puzzle piece.*)

PAUL: (*Pushing her hand away from his pieces:*) I'm doing the sky. (*He turns to* TOM) Alfred once was telling – . This must have been at my wedding. I'm not sure. He's teaching a class. (*Turns to* GEMMA:)

What's his field again?

GEMMA: The Romantics.

PAUL: So – say he was teaching – Shelley? Whatever. And a student stands up in the class and says: (*American*) 'What the hell does any of this have to do with my life? Why do I even have to listen to you? You worthless Englishman!! Don't you know you are nothing now? That you count for nothing in this world! This is our world! Get it?! So why don't you just shut up and listen!!' (*He laughs to himself.*)

TOM: He really – ?

PAUL: Something like that. I don't remember the exact words.

TOM: What did Alfred do?

(PAUL *looks to* GEMMA *who ignores him and continues to look over the puzzle.*)

PAUL: He didn't do anything. The students here grade their teachers, so Alfred says – you just have to take it.
(*The banging seems to have reached its climax upstairs. They listen, then it stops. Pause.*)

PAUL: (*Looking up at the ceiling:*) Silence. Dare we hope.
(*Standing, arms outstretched:*)
Thank you God! Maybe someone's finally come!!
(ELIZABETH *enters from the hallway in her robe.*)

ELIZABETH: (*Entering:*) Have you been hearing what's been going on upstairs? You can hear everything!

PAUL: They've stopped.

GEMMA: (*Under her breath:*) I wouldn't bet on it.

TOM: (To ELIZABETH:) How's the . . . (*He touches his stomach.*)

ELIZABETH: The medicine helped. Also the sleep, I think. I didn't know how tired I was.

PAUL: (*Looking at his watch:*) You only slept for – .

ELIZABETH: (*Interrupting, to* GEMMA:) Is that tea?

GEMMA: The water's still – .

ELIZABETH: (*On her way to the stove:*) Anyone else? (*She is gone. Beat.*)

GEMMA: Who can sleep?

PAUL: (*Over the puzzle:*) As long as Sophie can –

GEMMA: The light was on in your room. When I came down.
(*Beat.*)

PAUL: (*Without looking up from the puzzle:*) Then I better go. (*He doesn't move.*)
(*Beat.*)
I've got one: (*American*) 'The farther east you go – the more dead they are.' I swear I heard this. In California.
(*Silence. They work on the puzzle. Suddenly both* TOM *and* GEMMA *speak at the same time:*)
TOM: (*To* PAUL:) I hear that you – .
GEMMA: (*Same time, to* TOM:) I wanted to ask – .
(*They stop themselves.*)
TOM: Go ahead, what were you – ?
GEMMA: (*Over this:*) No, please. It was just – . What were you going to say?
(*Beat.*)
TOM: Remember your thought. I was only going to say that I understand you're going to sing tomorrow, Paul.
(PAUL *looks up.*)
What are you going to sing?
PAUL: Who said that?
TOM: Alfred thought – .
PAUL: I haven't sung in front of people in years.
TOM: You were a professional singer – ?
PAUL: I took classes. I wasn't bad. But it was clear I was destined for the chorus, so . . . I hadn't even thought of singing.
(*Beat.*)
(*To* GEMMA:) Think I should? What would father have thought – such a mediocre voice sending him off.
GEMMA: I think he's already gone. Do what you want.
(ELIZABETH *enters with her tea and a cookie which she has found and now eats.*)
ELIZABETH: (*Eating the cookie:*) I think it's sick. Up there. How do they get the nerve? And do they think we're deaf?
PAUL: (*Over the puzzle:*) So I'm not alone.
TOM: (*To* GEMMA:) What were you going to say – . Before – .
GEMMA: Oh right. It wasn't . . . I was going to ask – . (*She looks at her brother and sister.*) Don't get angry with me. (*To* TOM:) Since you were here – I'd like to know what happened yesterday.

46

ELIZABETH: Gemma, it's one in the morning – !

PAUL: You don't have to Tom, I apologize for my sister.

GEMMA: (*Over this:*) I mean – after. I understand what he did.
(*Beat.*)

Were there police? I feel like I'd like to know. Should know.
But if you don't want to – . It's not that important.
(*Pause. She goes back to the puzzle.*)

TOM: (*Remembering:*) The police did come. An ambulance. An
officer talked to me. To Alice. He was pretty nice. Younger
than me.
(*He smiles. No one is looking at him. They are doing the puzzle.*)
Alice was able to say she wasn't all that surprised, he'd been
depressed, and so . . . That made things – quicker.
(*Beat.*)

(*Trying to recall more:*) Some people from the ambulance
cleaned up the study a little bit. I don't know how much you
want to know?

ELIZABETH: (*Sitting down now, to get closer to the puzzle; to*
GEMMA:) Move over a little.

PAUL: (*To* ELIZABETH:) The sky is mine. Do all that pink rock.
(*Beat.*)

TOM: Before the police came, Alice and I just sat in the hall
outside the study. I wouldn't allow her to go back in. Once
I'd seen . . .
(*Beat.*)

I helped her wash her face. She had some blood . . . She'd
seen him do it – you knew that. So everything she does – . I
think we should remember that.
(*Beat.*)

I came in and she was just sobbing. I pulled her into the hall.
I called the police. They took out the body in a body bag; on
a stretcher. I drove Alice in her car to the hospital behind the
ambulance. I don't even have my license with me.
(*Beat.*)

A funeral director was called. We met him in a room of the
hospital. Alice liked him right away. He's about my age.
Maybe a little younger.
(*Beat.*)

I'm just trying to recall if there's anything . . . It was the funeral director who gave us the name of the woman who did most of the cleaning up. Alice – Elizabeth knows this – found a few places she'd missed. You couldn't stop her. I couldn't have done it. There was a stain on the floorboards she couldn't get out or she didn't have the stuff in the house to get out. So Elizabeth – .

ELIZABETH: (*Doing the puzzle:*) I moved the carpet from one of the bedrooms. It's in the study now.

TOM: Where I'm supposed to sleep. (*He laughs.*)

PAUL: (*Looking up:*) Tom shouldn't have to – .

GEMMA: (*Same time:*) We can't let him sleep – .

TOM: (*Over this:*) I can't sleep anyway, please! (*Pats the puzzle:*) I'll just stay up all night. I often do.
(*More 'banging' from upstairs.*)

PAUL: (*Looking up:*) Now – the other one has to come! Jesus Christ . . .
(*They all look back at the puzzle.*)

TOM: (*To GEMMA:*) Is that enough? Is there a specific thing . . . ?

ELIZABETH: (*Changing the subject:*) Who is this Alice anyway?

GEMMA: I thought you knew her from publishing – .

ELIZABETH: I'm asking Tom.
(*TOM is surprised by this.*)
He's her relative.

GEMMA: I think we've imposed upon Tom enough for – .

TOM: I don't mind. Let's see. Alice was married to my brother. I knew her then. I always thought she was one of the more alive people that I knew.
(*More banging from upstairs.*)
They seemed happy. My brother and – . One of those couples who seem to get along. Then he found someone else. I thought he acted in a real shitty way. I told her so. Is this the sort of thing – ?

ELIZABETH: It'll do.

TOM: We hadn't seen each other for a few years. We ran into each other a couple of weeks ago on Fifth Avenue, agreed to have lunch, had lunch. I'd just broken up with a girl.

GEMMA: Your wife?

48

TOM: (*Shaking his head:*) This was just a few weeks – .

GEMMA: Right. American? The girl.

TOM: That's right. Anyway Alice took pity on me, invited me up here for a weekend in the country.

(*Beat.*)

So I could relax.

(*The noise from above has stopped.*)

TOM: She's a good person. She's gone through a lot.

PAUL: Sh-sh!

(*Everyone listens.*)

Dare we hope that this unpleasant experience is now behind us?

ELIZABETH: I'd only met Alice a few times. I think it's the same with all of us. I don't know – there's my father's house. My father's funeral service. Calling my father's friends. She's everywhere, isn't she? That's what I was thinking about upstairs. That I don't know who she is. Or what she wants.

PAUL: What are you talking about?

ELIZABETH: Father has a lot of things in this house. That were his. Open your eyes, Paul. Just look at the situation we're in: she decides about the cremation. She tells us where to sleep.

GEMMA: I thought you helped with that.

ELIZABETH: I did my best. Look, I don't want to make a big deal about this. I don't mean it to be a big deal. It's just something I've been thinking about.

PAUL: What is? I don't understand.

(ELIZABETH *holds her stomach.*)

What's wrong?

ELIZABETH: I'm sure it was the eggroll. That's what I've been burping up. Forget it, Paul. Do your jigsaw. That's what you're interested in.

PAUL: I'm not interested in the jigsaw!

(SOPHIE *now enters from the hall. She wears a thin, translucent nightgown.*)

SOPHIE: Is no one going to sleep in this house? What night owls you Bakers are.

ELIZABETH: We got woken up by – .

SOPHIE: Me too. (*She yawns.*) What was that noise? Sounded like

49

a tree limb banging on the roof. Must have gotten windy all of a sudden. Is that tea?

ELIZABETH: There's still water in the kettle.

SOPHIE: (*Yawning.*) I'm half asleep. (*She puts her arms around* PAUL's *neck.*) How's the puzzle coming? I love puzzles. They're a complete waste of time. I like that. (*She kisses him on the head.*) What are you going to do, make me sleep alone all night? Your sisters can't be that interesting. (*She laughs.*) Just joking. I'll make myself some tea. Anyone else? (*As she leaves for the stove:*) I'm upstairs thinking: what do I have to do to get my husband to go to bed? (*She smiles, then as if another thought – she fans herself for a second with her nightgown.*) I put on a cooler nightgown. It was hot in the room. (*She goes.*)

ELIZABETH: You're not going to shut me up, Paul.

PAUL: (*Over this:*) Leave me alone. This is all I ask.

ELIZABETH: (*Over this:*) You never change!

GEMMA: (*Over this:*) I don't want to talk about this! I don't want to talk about this! I don't want to talk about this!

(ALICE *has entered in a robe and bare feet. She stands, startled to see everyone. Short pause.*)

ALICE: What's everyone . . . ? Do you know what time it is? I think it's – .

ELIZABETH: We're having tea.

(*No one knows what to say.* SOPHIE *comes in, having put on the kettle.*)

SOPHIE: The kettle's on.

ALICE: You too? What's going on?

SOPHIE: I was just telling everyone – there was a tree limb, banging against the roof. Did you hear it?

(*Beat.*)

You must have, Alice. It woke me up.

(*Beat.*)

ALICE: I did hear it. Thank you.

(*She goes to the table and picks up a bottle.*) Alfred wants a . . . drink. I ran into him – in the hall. I'd been asleep. And then I suppose the tree limb . . .

PAUL: Sounded like a very big limb.

(ALICE *yawns.*)

ALICE: I promised to bring this . . . He's waiting. Goodnight. Remember, tomorrow is going to be a long day as well. (*She turns to leave.*)

ELIZABETH: Alice, when do we decide who gets what?

PAUL: This is not the time – .

GEMMA: It's the middle of the night, Elizabeth!

ELIZABETH: I want to know!!

(*Beat.*)

ALICE: What's there to get?

ELIZABETH: There are chairs. Silverware. Plates. Photographs and frames. Books. Table.

ALICE: (*Turns away:*) Take what you want, Elizabeth.

ELIZABETH: (*Irrational now:*) How dare you speak to me like that!

GEMMA: Stop it, Elizabeth!

PAUL: (*Same time:*) Leave her alone!

ELIZABETH: I only want what is fair!! This was my father!! Do you understand that, woman?! So how are we going to divide his things?! What is so wrong with that question?! Do we divide into three? In four . . . ?

ALICE: Is that the question you're really trying to ask, Elizabeth?

ELIZABETH: (*To others:*) What is she talking about? Does she have ears?

ALICE: Is that what you want to ask me?!! Is it?!!!! Or do you want to know why I – . Do you think I didn't know you could hear?! I've lived in this house for two years and I know what can be heard!! But I didn't care! Why? Becuase I don't give one fuck what you – kids – think of me!! Why should I?!

ELIZABETH: (*Nearly in tears:*) I don't know why I'm listening to this. What have I done?

TOM: I think we should stop before – .

ELIZABETH: (To ALICE:) What you don't understand is I'm not interested in you, Alice. My question had to do with chairs, tables, there are lamps, rugs . . .

ALICE: He was so disappointed in all of you!!

ELIZABETH: (*Desperately trying to stay calm:*) Books, there's his car, garden equipment – .

TOM: (*Putting his hand on Elizabeth's arm:*) I think you should talk about all this in the morning.

ELIZABETH: (*Suddenly all of her anger comes out, directed at* TOM:)
Who the hell are you?! You little son-of-a-bitch, you don't
even belong here. This has nothing to do with you!! Shut up!
Shut up! Shut up!
(ELIZABETH *starts to sob. No one knows what to do. Pause.*)
TOM: I think I'll take a walk.
PAUL: Tom, she didn't mean – .
TOM: I know. I didn't take it personally. But I could use some air.
(*He goes out.* ELIZABETH *cries.*)
ALICE: I'm sorry. We'll discuss everything. The house – that was
your father's. It's yours. I have a few things . . . I'll make a
list of what they are. (*She sits and pours herself a drink.*
SOPHIE *goes to* ELIZABETH *and puts her arm around her.*)
SOPHIE: It's all right.
(*She pats* ELIZABETH. *Short pause.*)
ELIZABETH: I'm sorry about . . . (*Gestures toward where* TOM
exited.) But it really is none of his business. What is he doing
here anyway? (*She blows her nose.*
TOM *returns, unseen by anyone.*)
Alice said on our walk that she can't get rid of him. She
doesn't know why he stayed. He didn't even know father.
You'd think he'd know he didn't belong.
ALICE: I put him in the study for Christ sake. You'd think he'd
have taken the hint.
(*She laughs, as does* ELIZABETH. *Then slowly they realize* TOM *is
there and heard all this. No one knows what to say. Short pause.*)
TOM: It's – raining. Outside. Just started.
(*Beat.*)
I think I'll go to bed now. Goodnight. (*He goes.*)
(ELIZABETH *sniffles.* ALICE *takes a sip of her drink.*)
ALICE: I'm drunk.

SCENE 7

The kitchen. An hour later.
GEMMA *sits at the table, staring into space.* ELIZABETH *sits, going
through Harry's photo album which Alice had left on the table.*

From upstairs, we hear ALICE *screaming; the realization of what Harry did has hit her and she sounds like a wounded animal.*

GEMMA *and* ELIZABETH *pretend to ignore the screams.*

ALFRED *enters from the hallway, obviously upset. He wears only his underpants.*

ALFRED: (*Entering:*) Where's Alice's purse? Have you seen – ? (*Grabs the purse.*) Is this it? (*He opens it, digs around and pulls out a bottle of prescription pills.*)

(ALICE *screams again.*)

ELIZABETH: (*Looking through the album:*) Can't you do something?

ALFRED: It's all just hit her. She needs to sleep.

(*He goes back into the hall with the pills.* ALICE *screams again. Pause.*)

ELIZABETH: (*Holding the album:*) Look at this. I tell you there are pictures of us I've never even seen before. You must be no more than six.

(GEMMA, *distracted, nods.*)

Here's one of Paul.

(*Beat.*)

I'm thinking of keeping this. The whole thing.

GEMMA: Oh God, Liz – !

ELIZABETH: I want it. She can't know who half the people are.

GEMMA: She'll make you copies. It's Alice's! (*She reaches over the table for the album*)

ELIZABETH: (*Pushing her off; over this:*) She can't appreciate it like we can!

GEMMA: (*Over this:*) It's not yours to take!

(*They struggle over the album.*)

ELIZABETH: (*Over this:*) Let go! I want to take it!

GEMMA: (*Over this:*) Give it to me!!

(*Finally* GEMMA *gets the album.* TOM *has entered to see the end of this fight. He wears pajamas now.* ELIZABETH *and* GEMMA *breathe heavily for a moment.*)

ELIZABETH: (To GEMMA:) I don't understand you.

(*They notice* TOM *for the first time. Beat.*)

TOM: (*To* ELIZABETH:) I'm still here. Sorry. There's no bus service at two o'clock in the morning.

(*He crosses the room and goes off to the sink.* GEMMA *sighs.*)

GEMMA: What that man must think of us.

ELIZABETH: Who cares?

(*She gets up and leaves. Beat.*)

GEMMA: (*After her:*) Goodnight, Liz! Goodnight.

(*Beat.* TOM *enters, on his way back to the hall. He carries a roll of paper towels.*)

GEMMA: (*As he passes her:*) So – you teach acting.

(*He stops.*)

That must be very interesting. I love the theatre. In London I used to go all the time. I remember when I first came to the States – .

TOM: Gemma. I'm tired.

GEMMA: (*Over this:*) Uncle Alfred had invited me – . I grabbed at the chance. I needed to get away. Perhaps like you needed to get away from New York and come up here – .

TOM: (*Turns:*) Alice invited me for this weekend. I didn't ask to come.

GEMMA: I'm sure she did, I didn't mean – .

TOM: I had to get out of quite a few other commitments. It wasn't easy.

GEMMA: No.

TOM: I had other places I could have gone to. And then when – your father . . . What the hell was I supposed to do?! I would have felt like I was abandoning – .

GEMMA: (*Over this:*) You don't have to explain.

TOM: (*Continuing:*) I couldn't even get to the bus station. Alice wasn't going to take me. How could I ask – ? I told her I'd only be in the way. With all of you coming – . I asked her to let me leave. You think I'd want to put myself through – ?! (*Stops himself. Short pause.*)

GEMMA: Thank God you stayed. You've been such a help.

TOM: I'm not hurt. I'm fine. You don't have to say anything. (*Beat.*)

There's a bus at nine. I found a schedule in your father's desk.

(*Pause.*)

GEMMA: What were we – ? The theatre.

54

TOM: Gemma.

GEMMA: Anyway, I arrived here and I saw a show in New York. And there was this actor, long hair down to – , almost growling, spitting as he talked. I remember thinking, is this acting? The growling, I mean. Then after about a year of living in the States, I began to realize I could not imagine there was anything else. Why do you have all those paper towels?

TOM: Alfred got sick in the study. Remember?

GEMMA: And no one cleaned – ?

TOM: (*Over this:*) I don't mind!

(*Beat.*)

GEMMA: What you must think of us.

TOM: (*What has been on his mind:*) About the cremation, Gemma. Alice said to me – before any of you got here, when she had no one else to talk to – she said that Harry probably would not have wanted to be cremated. But it was something she believed in, so – she went ahead and did it.

(*Beat.*)

She asked me if I thought that was okay.

(*Beat.*)

I don't mean to criticize Alice. But someone should know, I thought. Not that there's anything you can do about it now. I'm only saying, that sometimes Alice can say one thing to you and another thing to me. I wanted you to know that.

(*Beat.*)

For Christ sake go to bed. (*He turns to leave.*)

GEMMA: (*Desperate:*) So where in London do you come from, Tom?

(*Beat. He stops. From upstairs* ALICE *screams a few times, still like a wounded animal.*)

Where did you live?

TOM: Chiswick.

GEMMA: That's not too far from – . Do you know Eel Brook Common? In Fulham, off the King's – .

TOM: A friend of mine and I used to play tennis there.

GEMMA: My God, he knows our common!

TOM: There's a court – .

GEMMA: Two! And a playground. It's not a very big common. Not that many people know it, in London.

TOM: Why should they!

(*Beat.*)

GEMMA: (*Half to herself:*) That common is so close to where we lived!

(*He turns to go.*)

Tom! Ever since we got here, I've been wanting to tell someone.

(*He stops to listen.*)

I've got good news! I've been looking for the chance to . . .

(*Beat.*)

I'm engaged.

(*He turns back to her. Short pause.*)

TOM: Congratulations – .

GEMMA: He's American!

TOM: Why are you telling me – ?

GEMMA: Like your girlfriend!

(*Beat.*)

TOM: I'm sure your family would be very interested in – .

GEMMA: He's from New Mexico. He's even part Mexican, but his family has been here – . Years and years.

TOM: (*Over this:*) Why do I care about your – ?

(ALICE *screams in the distance. This stops them both.*)

GEMMA: (*Referring to the scream:*) What a night. She's realized what she's lost. She's scared. God, let her sleep. (*She turns back to* TOM:) My fiance. He's big, you think of them as small – the Mexicans, but not him. He's tall.

(*Beat.*)

Can't read worth a damn though. (*Laughs to herself.*) Can't read at all, I think. He's my gardener. Or works for the man who does my garden. He doesn't know shit about art, music . . . As thick as a brick shithouse, his expression. A big dumb American like you see at the beach.

(*Beat.*)

I love the way he feels. His body. And he's a nice man. Warm. Open.

(*Short pause.*)

When I told father – he went crazy. He said – (*She laughs to herself.*) What the hell is wrong with me?
(*Beat.*)
He said – he'd given me culture. He'd educated me. He'd taught me right from wrong. I don't know what that had to do with – . But it's what he said. Good from evil. Beauty from ugliness. And now – I do this – terrible thing. I told him he wasn't being fair. At least he should meet – . But he just kept screaming at me: 'Where have we gone wrong?' 'Where have we gone wrong?'
(*Beat.*)
'How did we all get to here?'
(*Beat.*)
I didn't understand. But I'd never heard him shout like that – not at me.
(*Beat.*)
'The barbarians are sweeping over us and all we do is kiss their ass.' His words. I don't know what they mean.
(*Beat.*)
I tried to get him to calm down. Usually I could find a way, but this time it was impossible. It just kept coming out. The anger. At everything. At me . . . I warned him, Tom – if he did anything to himself, I'd hate him forever!
(*Short pause.*)
This was yesterday – this conversation. When I called – he was in his study. He'd been reading he said and – I could hear – listening to music.

TOM: Yesterday afternoon?
(*Short pause.*)

GEMMA: At first, when Alice phoned with the news – I blamed myself. I even thought *I'd* killed him.
(*Beat.*)
I know that's unfair to me. I did nothing wrong. I was one thing maybe – a final straw to someone's . . . problem. It's taken me until now – to accept that it really had nothing to do with me.
(*A single scream from* ALICE *in the distance.*)
(*To* TOM:) Did it?

TOM: No. I'm sure it didn't.

GEMMA: (*Suddenly relieved:*) I've put myself through so much today. (*She stands.*) He should have been happy, dammit! With my news! I tried to tell him, Tom – we change. You have to. (*She starts to leave.*) Thank you. I'll try and go to sleep now. Goodnight. (*She goes.*)

TOM: Goodnight.

(*Short pause.* TOM *hesitates, then picks up the roll of paper towels he'd set on the table, and he too heads into the hall, as* ALICE *screams again.*)

SCENE 8

The kitchen. Morning.

ALICE, ALFRED, GEMMA, ELIZABETH *and* SOPHIE *are sitting at the table. The men are in black suits, the women in black dresses. Two or three are drinking coffee. The table has been cleared of the papers, etc. and is very neat. In the centre of the table is an urn – Harry's ashes.*

SOPHIE: (*telling a story:*) There's a man – he's American of course. And he's standing in line to get into Buckingham Palace.

ALFRED: For the tour?

SOPHIE: (*She nods:*) And he asks the guard, (*American*) 'When will we see the Queen?' The guard says she's in Scotland. The man is beside himself, he says, 'The Queen should be here! When I go to Disneyland Mickey's there!' (*She laughs loudly, the others smile politely.*) My daughter told me that.

ALFRED: (*To no one:*) Speaking of Disneyland, at least we don't have one stuck in the middle of our country. (*He laughs.*)

ALICE: Anyone want more coffee?

(PAUL *enters, also in a black suit.*)

PAUL: (*Entering:*) He's going to stay.

ALICE: Thank Heaven!

ALFRED: (*Same time:*) I would think – .

GEMMA: (*Same time:*) To leave now.

ELIZABETH: (*Same time:*) Who did he think was going to take him to the station?

(*Beat.*)

58

ALICE: And Harry's suit?

ELIZABETH: (*To Alice:*) What about father's – ?

ALICE: (*Over this:*) He hadn't brought a suit, of course. He was coming for a weekend!

PAUL: I rolled up the cuffs. He'll be okay. (*He sits.*)

SOPHIE: (*To* PAUL:) I told them about the Queen and Mickey Mouse. They found it very funny.

ALICE: Thank God, it's a beautiful day. Did anyone else see the sunrise this morning, or was I the only one up?
(TOM *enters, wearing one of Harry's black suits which is a few sizes too large. The others look at him.*)

TOM: (*After a moment:*) I don't want to look foolish.
(*No response.*)

GEMMA: Sit down and have some coffee. Make room – . Let Tom sit . . .

TOM: (*Sitting:*) I didn't even bring a tie.

ALFRED: (*To* TOM:) I never got to hear all your accents. I hear you do a very funny midwest. Our Dean's from the midwest.
(*Laughs to himself.*)

TOM: I don't think I feel like – .

ALFRED: I had a student stand up in class once, and say, (*American*) 'You're nothing. Shut up!' (*Laughs.*)

TOM: Paul told me the story – .

ALFRED: He had a midwest accent.

ALICE: We were just saying – it's a beautiful day.

GEMMA: It's not going to rain.

TOM: It rained last night.

ALFRED: Did it? When we went for our walk – .

TOM: Later. I stepped out for a moment. And it was raining. Then I came back in. The guests are due in . . . ? (*He looks at his watch.*)

ALICE: If you see a young woman, blonde, very attractive – Harry's star pupil, the violinist – snub her.
(*Short pause.*)
I'm terrible with names. Everyone – if I don't introduce you . . .
(*Pause.* TOM *notices the urn.*)

TOM: Is that the . . . ?

ALICE: I picked it up this morning. It was waiting for me. Do you
    want to look inside?

TOM: I don't think I need – .

ALICE: (*To everyone:*) The man at the funeral home, not the
    funeral director, but the little man who sits by the guest book
    – I think he works there. Anyway, he said to be sure, that
    when we throw the ashes – to keep our mouths closed.
    (*Others turn away.*)
    It's good advice!
    (*Beat.*)
    Obviously there'd been a bad experience . . .

SOPHIE: (*Standing and collecting the cups:*) If we're not going to
    have anymore cof – .

GEMMA: Tom never got – .

TOM: (*Over this:*) I'm fine.
    (*Short pause as* SOPHIE *carries the cups to the sink [off].*)

ELIZABETH: (*To* GEMMA:) Did you know that father called her –
    Fifi?

ALICE: (*Nodding to the urn:*) They had a catalogue. I had no idea
    what Harry'd want. I picked that one out. It's nice, isn't it?
    (*Everyone quickly agrees that the urn is nice.*)
    A couple were quite gawdy. (*She shrugs.*)
    (GEMMA *notices* ELIZABETH *looking at something on her lap.*)

GEMMA: (*To* ELIZABETH:) What are you looking at?

ELIZABETH: (*Holding up the photo album:*) Has everyone seen
    these photos – ?
    (GEMMA *grabs the album and hands it to* ALICE.)

GEMMA: Maybe you could make a few copies for us.

ALICE: Just say which ones you want.

GEMMA: Thank you.
    (ALICE *starts to look through the album.* SOPHIE *returns from the
    sink, and goes and stands behind* PAUL, *putting her hands on his
    shoulders.*)

PAUL (*To everyone:*) Excuse me, if we have a minute . . . Sophie
    and I'd like to clear something up.
    (*Beat.*)
    Yesterday – and God it was only yesterday when we arrived,
    wasn't it? (*Shakes his head in amazement.*) When Sophie and I

arrived – . Elizabeth. Well, Sophie felt that you – . When she came up to you to hug you? To console you? She says you turned away from her and ran to hug me.

ELIZABETH: Oh God! I don't remember – .

PAUL: I didn't exactly see this either, but she says – .

SOPHIE: (*To* ELIZABETH:) You sort of pushed me away – to get to Paul.

PAUL: And this hurt Sophie. Correct? But Elizabeth, you didn't mean to hurt her. That too is correct?

ELIZABETH: No. Of course – . Why would I – ?

PAUL: (*To* SOPHIE:) There. That has been addressed and dealt with.
(*Beat.*)

ELIZABETH: (*Needing to explain:*) I saw my brother. I wanted to hug him.

SOPHIE: (*Wanting help:*) Paul.

PAUL: My Sophie is your sister-in-law. She wanted to console you. She wanted to be consoled herself. You should have let her do that. She has feelings too. Our father's death – upset her as well. Is that right, Sophie?

SOPHIE: Maybe this isn't the time to bring this up . . .

PAUL: You asked me – !

SOPHIE: (*Interrupting:*) But I'm sure your sisters want to know these things.
(*Beat.*)

ALICE: (*Quietly, showing Alfred a photo in the album:*) Harry bought me this bathing suit. (*She looks at* ALFRED, *then at everyone else.*) I hope I didn't keep anyone awake last night. Alfred thinks it must have been either the eggrolls or the moo-shoo pork. What do you think?

PAUL: (*Putting his arm around Sophie:*) She had just a bite of the moo-shoo and – .

GEMMA: (*Over this:*) Elizabeth – .

ELIZABETH: (*Over this:*) The eggrolls definitely!

PAUL: If we were Americans we'd sue!
(*He laughs, others laugh. Beat.*)

ALFRED: None of you probably know this, but last night – Alice and I had the chance to spend some time together.

(*Others look down.*)
To talk.

ALICE: We'd hardly known each other before. We'd only met the – .

ALFRED: One time. At Paul's wedding.

ALICE: Paul and Sophie's wedding.

ALFRED: Alice couldn't make your mother's funeral.

ALICE: I sent flowers.

ALFRED: The one time. (*He looks at her.*) I have asked Alice to come to Albuquerque.

ALICE: To visit!

GEMMA: (*Over this:*) That's wonderful! And maybe even stay – .

ALICE: I don't think – .

ALFRED: Wait until she sees the colours!

GEMMA: Uncle Alfred's right – it's the colours, they'll shock you – they're lunar, that's how I describe them.
(*Beat.*)
Alfred says they're vaginal.
(*All except* PAUL *and* ELIZABETH *laugh.*)

PAUL: (*To himself:*) I suppose we see what we want to see.
(*Beat.*)

ELIZABETH: And what will you do about the house?

GEMMA: Elizabeth, we said we'd talk – .

ALICE: Close it? Sell it?
(*Beat.*)
And go West! That's what Americans are always doing, isn't it? At least for a visit.
(*Beat.*)
I assume you want me to sell it. No one wants to live here . . . ?
(*Beat.*)

GEMMA: We'll talk this afternoon – about the things.

ELIZABETH: Or tomorrow. (*To* PAUL:) Are you still flying back tomorrow?

PAUL: We can't stay – .

SOPHIE: (*Over this:*) Claire – .

GEMMA: I'm going back tonight.

ELIZABETH: Tonight! You didn't say – .

GEMMA: Into New York. I'm seeing friends. I'm hardly ever east
  anymore.
PAUL: (*To* GEMMA:) Tom's on the bus this afternoon – .
TOM: Alfred was going to drive me into town – .
GEMMA: (*To* TOM:) I can drive you all the way in if you don't
  mind waiting until – .
TOM: The bus is fine. I have the ticket.
  (*Beat.*)
ELIZABETH: (*To* PAUL:) You're still here tonight.
  (PAUL *nods. Beat.*)
PAUL: Thanksgiving's in a month. Do we celebrate Thanks – ?
ALICE: Sh-sh!
  (*Everyone is silent.* ALICE *gets up and looks outside.*)
  I thought I heard . . .
SOPHIE: (*To* PAUL:) Are they late?
  (ALICE, *who has been holding a book, opens it. She looks up.*)
ALICE: If anyone asks, don't say anything about the college. Or if
  you do say Harry loved teaching there. Don't say the truth.
  (*Beat.*)
  (*Looking at the book:*) I thought, this was . . . right. Do you
  mind? You'll hear it twice.
  (*Everyone:* 'No!' 'Of course not!' 'Please.' ALICE *looks at the
  urn.*)
  Once, only for the family, Harry.
  (*She reaches and turns the urn so it 'faces' her. She reads* [*from
  Keats's* Ode on Melancholy]*:*)
    'But when the melancholy fit shall fall
      Suddenly from heaven like a weeping cloud,
    That fosters the droop-headed flowers all,
      And hides the green hills in an April shroud;
    Then glut thy sorrow on a morning rose,
      Or on the rainbow of the salt sand-wave,
        Or on the wealth of globed peonies;
    Or if thy mistress some rich anger shows,
      Emprison her soft hand and let her rave,
        And feed deep, deep upon her peerless eyes.
    She dwells with Beauty – Beauty that must die.'
  (*Pause. She closes the book.*)

GEMMA: Father.

(*Short pause.*)

ELIZABETH: Paul? For the family? What did you plan to sing?

(PAUL *hesitates.*)

ALFRED: Come on, Paul.

(*He slowly stands.*)

PAUL: I didn't know what to choose.

GEMMA: (To TOM:) Have you ever heard him sing?

TOM: No, I – ?

GEMMA: Come on, break our hearts. I haven't started to cry yet.
You might as well get me going.

PAUL: I haven't sung in front of people for – .

ELIZABETH: Why is it we have to apologize for everything?!!

(*Beat.*)

PAUL: Okay. 'Those of us who knew my father well' – this is my
introduction – 'knew my father well, will always associate
this piece – with him. For you – Father. May you now have
the peace you sought.'

(*Beat. He begins to sing: 'The British Grenadiers'.*)

'Some talk of Alexander,
And some of Hercules,
Of Hector and Lysander,
And such great names as these . . . '

(*With the first line the family bursts out laughing.*)

GEMMA: (*Over the singing:*) Great choice!!

ELIZABETH: (*Over this:*) He'd love it!!

GEMMA: (*To* TOM:) Father used to sing this while he shaved! It
drove us crazy!

ALICE: He still does! Did!!

PAUL: (*Continuing:*)

'But of all the world's brave heroes,
There's none that can compare,
With a tow, row, row row, row,
Row, to the British Grenadiers!'

(*All except* TOM *try to sing along, banging the table to the march
beat.*)

EVERYONE: 'Whene'er we are commanded
To storm the Palisades,

Our leaders march with fuses,
And we with hand grenades.'
ALICE: (*To* TOM:) Don't you know it?
TOM: A little.
GEMMA: Then sing!
EVERYONE: 'We throw them from thé glacis,
About the enemies ears,
With a tow, row, row, row, row,
Row, the – '
SOPHIE: (*Shouts out:*) French!!!
EVERYONE: 'British Grenadiers!!!'
(*The family suddenly sings in a whisper, obviously as* HARRY *used to do it:*)
EVERYONE: (*Whispering:*)
'And when the siege is over,
We to the town repair,
The townsmen cry – .
(*The family shout:*)
'Hurrah boys, here comes a Grenadier;
Here comes the – .'
ALICE: Sh-sh!!!
(*They stop singing. Beat.* ALICE *goes and looks out.*)
It's a car. The guests are arriving.
(*Pause.* ALICE *takes out a cigarette, lights it; takes one puff and puts it out.*
Everyone is straightening their clothes. TOM *tries to straighten his.*)
SOPHIE: (*To* TOM:) You look good.
ELIZABETH: Paul, you better direct traffic. Tell everyone where to park.
(*He nods.*)
GEMMA: I can take their coats.
ELIZABETH: Put them upstairs.
PAUL: I thought it was outside – .
ELIZABETH: Until everyone comes.
(*They are on their way out.*)
ALICE: Just one thing I meant to tell you.
(*They stop.*)

65

You should know this.

(*Beat.*)

When people called – I told them, it had just been an accident. That Harry was cleaning his gun.

(*She heads down the hall. The others look at each other and follow;* GEMMA *tries to straighten out* TOM'*s suit as they go. The urn is left alone on the table.*

Debussy's The Girl with the Flaxen Hair *begins to play.*

Off, the sound of greetings, condolences, cars arriving, offers to take coats, car doors closing, directions where to park, etc.)